HR'S GREATEST CHALLENGE

Driving the C-Suite to Improve Employee Engagement and Retention

RICHARD P. FINNEGAN

HR'S GREATEST CHALLENGE

Driving the C-Suite to Improve Employee Engagement and Retention

RICHARD P. FINNEGAN

Society for Human Resource Management

Alexandria, VA

shrm.org

Society for Human Resource Management, India Office

Mumbai, India

shrmindia.org

Society for Human Resource Management

Haidian District Beijing, China

shrm.org/cn

Society for Human Resource Management, Middle East and Africa Office

Dubai, UAE

shrm.org/pages/mena.aspx

Founded in 1948, the Society for Human Resource Management (SHRM) is the world's largest HR membership organization devoted to human resource management. Representing more than 275,000 members in over 160 countries, the Society is the leading provider of resources to serve the needs of HR professionals and advance the professional practice of human resource management. SHRM has more than 575 affiliated chapters within the United States and subsidiary offices in China, India and United Arab Emirates. Visit us at shrm.org.

Interior and Cover Design: Mari Adams

Library of Congress Cataloging-in-Publication Data
Finnegan, Richard P.
  HR's greatest challenge : driving the C-suite to improve employee engagement and retention / Richard P. Finnegan.
     pages cm
Includes bibliographical references and index.
ISBN 978-1-58644-379-5
1. Employee motivation. 2. Employee attitude surveys. 3. Employee retention. I. Title.
HF5549.5.M63F557 2015
658.3'14--dc23
                    2015001929

15-0038

Contents

For Bob Bowen, retired HR exec and my best boss ever, who earned my trust on our first day together when he said, "The only thing that exceeds my lack of knowledge about benefits is my lack of interest."

Thank you, Bob, for making me smarter over the past 30 years of our friendship. My life is better for knowing you, and I am forever grateful.

Introduction:
A C-Word Lesson from China

This is a book about new ideas. The purpose is to help executive-level HR professionals improve engagement and retention for their organizations by leveraging the immense power of their CEOs, CFOs, and other C-suite executives. The value proposition in one sentence is: *Since organizations have developed successful processes for sales and service, let's apply these same successful processes for employee engagement and retention.*

Naming this book *HR's Greatest Challenge* might seem bold compared to other obstacles you face each day, but data presented throughout this book and particularly in Chapter 3 will convince you this is true.

Improving engagement and retention in the same ways you address sales and service might seem logical, intuitive, and easy, but you will soon learn that the great majority of organizations operate nearly opposite of this way. One reason why is because they have all followed each other to buy surveys, implement programs, and measure their outcomes against their peers'. I will show you a better way that is indeed logical and intuitive, but not initially easy.

This book will challenge every aspect of traditional thinking organizations apply to employee engagement and retention. Doing what I suggest here requires moving these critical metrics and their associated sky-high dollar values from the isolation of HR departments into the minute-to-minute management mainstream of modern organizations, a mainstream hyper-driven by CEOs and steered by the metrics handed to them by their CFOs. Incorporating employee engagement and retention into this business mainstream and including these metrics as top-5 for boards of directors and executives is long, long overdue.

Because this book brings fresh thinking, I urge you to consider your own willingness to push both yourself and your C-suite colleagues outside of your comfort zones. "Fresh thinking" sounds intriguing until it challenges our own beliefs and threatens the way we currently do our work. Stronger alerts come when we see we must influence others to change their thinking too, when many of them tower over us on the organization chart.

We have all learned that the critical strength of HR executives who participate meaningfully in their organizations is that they think strategically, connect their people-management smarts to business outcomes, and ultimately cause their executive teams to follow. Read on if true leadership and smart pioneering come easy to you, but save your receipt to return this book if not.

The steepness of this challenge was first brought home to me over dinner in a foreign land. Mark Jin is the top executive for the HR Excellence Center of China. My company partners with Mark to improve retention and engagement for his client companies in China including Microsoft, AstraZeneca, Coca-Cola, and Rolls Royce. Most of these companies are multinationals that are ambitiously chasing dollars—or yuan, the Chinese currency—in the world's largest marketplace.

Mark has a way with words, perhaps because he brings a rare combination of western business savvy with sharp cultural recognition of what works in China. Or maybe it is his Chinese upbringing that causes him to say short sentences that have profound meaning unlike anyone else I know. Mark can be downright movie-like.

The Chinese turnover problem extends way past the typical question: "They have 1.3 billion people, so how can they run out of workers?" Most westerners think of Chinese employees as laborers assembling cellphones in football-field size factories, and for sure China has many of these factories. Worker shortages, though, stem from Chinese laws that limit the number of professional workers who can enter from other countries and from the high taxes for paying them. These laws increase the likelihood that Chinese citizens who are managers, salespeople, researchers, scientists, accountants, lawyers, doctors, HR executives, and other professionals all have jobs. And there are plenty of jobs.

The ever-expanding Shanghai skyline resembles one giant architecture contest. With bragging rights for some of the world's tallest buildings, these structures are not occupied each day by cellphone-makers but instead by Chinese professionals. And the continuing onslaught of multinational companies chasing the yuan guarantees more and more opportunities for a limited number of professional Chinese. It is typical for a 30-year-old Chinese engineer to tell a story like, "My grandfather was a farmer. My father works for the state. I will work wherever I want."

And if that person wants to make a lot of money, he or she should become a headhunter. Turnover in China is such an expensive problem that the concept of employee engagement is hardly mentioned at all.

During our first dinner together in Shanghai, Mark listened carefully to how we help client companies cut turnover in the western half of the world. He heard terms like "goals," "accountabilities," and "leaders owning their talent." I presented ideas such as putting dollar costs on turnover and designing fresh-thinking reports that elevate both retention and engagement from second-tier metrics to first-tier metrics—the ones CFOs study along with HR—in other words, converting retention and engagement from HR issues to highly regarded business issues. Mark paused when I finished, and then said these words: "*For HR executives to do this, they must have courage.*"

I have reflected on this discussion many times. One cannot-miss conclusion is that our client companies that have shown the most improvement in turnover and engagement are ones that the CEOs readily accepted and put the contents of this book into practice. In some cases the CEOs immediately saw the difference between our business-driven methods and the ineffective strategies companies use like exit surveys, traditional engagement surveys, and superficial manager and employee programs. These CEOs then convinced others around the executive table to abandon long-held assumptions and to attack retention and engagement through leader accountability.

Mark's words also reminded me of companies that heard our approach and declined to move forward because of the two most common objections: "not part of our culture" or "leaders don't have time." These companies refuse to think reflectively and to take a crowbar to their ineffective ways.

I commit that when you finish reading this book you will have every bit of data and every tool you need to gain the lost money slipping through your fingers. My goal, though, is higher than to give you data. I will compel you to act. Our company has worked onsite on all six inhabited continents and has successfully applied the solutions you will read here. We know these ideas work.

Dick Finnegan
Longwood, Florida

Part I: Challenges

Chapter 1.

The Dollar Values
of Engagement and Retention
Merit Top-5 Metric Status

True story. Not long ago I met with the recruiting manager for a global engineering company in the lobby of a Walt Disney World hotel. Every reader of this book would immediately recognize this company's name. This gentleman's responsibility is to locate and hire talent for 57,000 positions across the U.S., and most of these jobs require technical skills.

Let's call this man William. William said he brought his recruiting team to Florida to strategize hiring for the next five years, to align it with his company's strategic plan. Acknowledging that I was there to talk about retention, our discussion flowed like this:

Me: I'm surprised you have enough internal talent to fill your expected openings, given your company's size as well as expansion and normal attrition.

William: Oh, we don't for sure, especially for expansion.

Me: So how can you plan a full five years out? How many blank spots are on your future organizational chart?

William: We have no blank spots, Dick. Our reason for coming here was to identify who will fill every spot.

Me: How can you identify enough specific talent to do that?

William: When you add the tools headhunters have used for years to the advantages offered by LinkedIn and other social media sites, it's quite easy. We've identified exactly who we intend to hire and have even moved their names onto our future charts.

Me: You've placed names of people who work for competitors onto your organizational charts?

William (laughing): Remember, we're a technology company, so that's easy. We spent most of our time identifying who we want, when we want them, and how we will take them.

Me: Are you sure you can "take them?"

William: Yes, we will take them.

This tale reinforces that sharks are circling your technology talent by the hour. If you have courage, ask your best performers how many headhunter calls they receive in a month, or even in a week.

This tale also reflects how engagement and retention drive profitability in ways that are both direct and indirect, obvious and subtle, and more visible to those who have either great vision or convincing data.

When I think about the my discussion with William, I stumble on this question: How many total dollars will be gained and lost as a result of this one meeting in a Disney World hotel? This company will now raid competing companies for specifically targeted talent over the next five years, and, assuming success, those companies will then raid other companies, and so on and so on. Consideration must be given to *the big numbers*, the ones exponentially larger than recruiting and replacement costs on both sides. How many dollars in profitability will be increased and decreased as these mountains of technical talent relocate? How many new products will be rushed to market while others lag due to unfilled technology positions? The total price tag will likely reach one billion dollars or more. And there will be winners and losers.

And all of this is because of one company's workforce planning meeting. How many other meetings are happening identical to this one across our world?

Imperfect Metrics

Turnover and engagement are, for sure, imperfect metrics. Leaders who must clear out deadwood will have high turnover rates for the good of their companies. Some employees quit for totally uncontrollable reasons such as when a parent becomes ill, and they must relocate to their home towns. Engagement tanks at times due to major layoffs when surviving employees wonder if any achievements can save their jobs. But though imperfect, engagement and retention join productivity outcomes as the best metrics for gauging how effectively leaders manage their talent—and thus the future of their businesses. A good comparison is the blood tests we all take as part of routine physical exams. When compared to baseline data, these tests tell our doctors how healthy we appear compared to the standards for good health. Sometimes doctors ask for additional tests, or data, because they spot an initial negative outcome. That is how engagement and retention data need to be managed. If you see a bad trend, investigate to learn more.

The challenge for this chapter is, how do we convince your C-suite executives that engagement and retention represent such substantial power in our organizations that they deserve top-5 metric status? That engagement and retention drive profitability, revenue, service levels, and safety levels? That engagement and retention merit serious and urgent rather than passive discussion during executive meetings and board meetings? That our CFOs should begin connecting the dots between these metrics and the metrics they consider to be most critical, so they can report engagement and retention as contributing factors or even cause-and-effect when describing financial trends and potential solutions? And most importantly, that executives can hold managers accountable in meaningful ways for engaging and retaining their teams? With *real* accountability?

I suspect that a few HR executives need convincing, too. We have been raised for decades conducting hamster-on-wheel activities like annual engagement surveys, resulting manager action plans, "survey-results" e-mails to employees, and exit surveys that yield questionable data and rarely any action. Many have watched their executives say lip-service phrases about how important their employees are to the company but who 30 days later disregard engagement survey results and give little thought to following up on managers' action plans. Living these activities year to year can easily cause us to reduce our own expectations and to fall in line with those who lack clear vision. Then as a result we see disengagement and turnover as rush-hour traffic, something we must accept and try to find ways to work around rather than to actually solve.

So you be the CEO, or, in this case, the jury. I will show you evidence—exhibits—to convince you that engagement and retention merit top-5 metric status.

Exhibit A: Let's Call Them Driving-Force Metrics

Let's concede from the start that we cannot compete with first-thing-CEOs-look-at-each-morning metrics. These are the traditional bottom-line numbers that CEOs check with coffee in hand, such as sales numbers in product companies, revenue and quality metrics in service companies, census in hospitals, and production in manufacturing. We are also severely handicapped because engagement and retention are not measured daily like other key metrics. So our goal becomes convincing our CEOs that employee engagement and retention drive these bottom-line numbers.

Before racing on to correlative data, though, let's make one simple appeal for common sense. Studies tell us that on average nearly 70 percent of all operating expenses go to paying and supporting our workforces.[1] Doesn't it seem right, then, that retaining and getting the most work out of this huge expense warrants top-5 attention? And if not, then why not?

But let us proceed to identify the numbers of dollars on the table rather than to ask our CEOs to put their full faith behind what we intuitively know, that engagement and retention drive those other metrics that our CEOs see as most important.

Fortunately, much work is available to solve this challenge. Most of us see Gallup as the world's survey leader, having gathered employee survey data from more than 25 million respondents in 189 countries and in 69 languages.[2] In its *State of the American Workplace* report,[3] Gallup shared the following about engagement data and correlations to those same metrics your CEO checks each morning.

When comparing companies' engagement levels for the top 25 percent of Gallup's survey database to the bottom 25 percent, *the more engaged groups* showed the following improvements:

- Profitability, 22 percent.
- Productivity, 21 percent.
- Customer ratings, 10 percent.
- Quality defects, 41 percent.
- Safety incidents, 48 percent.
- Patient safety incidents, 41 percent.
- Absenteeism, 37 percent.
- Shrinkage, 28 percent.

I sequenced these data based on my estimates of which are most valuable to your CEO. But if the data told us only that profitability increased by 22 percent, shouldn't that be sufficient evidence to convince? The remaining findings all contribute to that profitability increase.

As importantly, Gallup observed that employers with high engagement have much higher sticking power too. Turnover was lower by 65 percent in what Gallup classified as low-turnover organizations and 25 percent in high-turnover organizations. And Gallup went on to say that all of these correlations are highly consistent across different organizations from diverse industries and regions of the world.

But *more* importantly, Gallup reported that companies with engaged workforces have higher earnings per share, or EPS, and seem to have recovered from the recession at a faster rate. Specifically, organizations with an average of 9.3 engaged employees for every actively disengaged employee experienced a 147 percent higher EPS compared with their competition. This is one of those "wow" metrics that should resound around every C-suite! In contrast, organizations with an average of 2.6 engaged employees for every actively disengaged employee experienced 2 percent lower EPS compared with their competition during that same period.

Gallup segmented surveyed employees into "engaged," "not engaged," and "actively disengaged," and summarized with the following:

Engaged employees are the ones who are the most likely to drive the innovation, growth, and revenue that their companies desperately need. These engaged workers build new products and services, generate new ideas, create new customers, and ultimately help spur the economy to create more good jobs.[4]

Actively disengaged employees cost the U.S. between $450 billion and $550 billion each year in lost productivity. They are more likely to steal from their companies, negatively influence their coworkers, miss workdays, and drive customers away.[5]

Based on these definitions, is it any surprise, then, that clusters of engaged employees create more profitability than actively disengaged employees?

Exhibit B: *Fortune* Top 100

The Great Place to Work Institute is the survey company that drives the *Fortune* magazine's "100 Best Companies to Work For®" lists along with similar "best places to work" lists across 45 countries. A review of the institute's database of "over 10 million employee voices" revealed the following:

- » Committed and engaged employees who trust their management perform 20 percent better than other employees.[6]
- » Companies with committed and engaged employees have as much as 65 percent less voluntary turnover compared to their competitors.[7]
- » The financial performance of the publicly traded companies on the *Fortune* 100 Best Companies list consistently outperform major stock indices by 300 percent.[8]

Pictures do speak louder than words when presenting evidence to our CEO jury. Figure 1.1 sits on the Great Place to Work's website and represents the extreme earnings-per-share gap between companies that earn a place on the institute's lists versus companies that do not. I will discuss the criteria for Great Place to Work's lists later in Chapter 3.

Figure 1.1 Comparative Cumulative Stock Market Returns

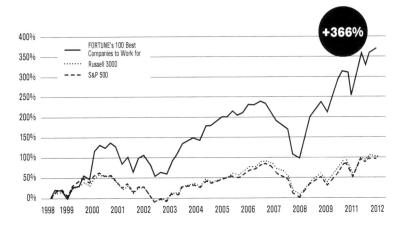

Exhibit C: Engagement Drives Sales

Towers Perrin looked at engagement results for over 32,000 employees across dozens of companies and found a positive relationship between engagement and sales growth, lower cost of goods sold, customer focus, and reduced turnover.[9]

Northwestern University professors researched the impact of sales personnel's extra efforts on customer spending. They found when salespeople give just 10 percent more effort, customers tend to spend 22.7 percent more.[10]

Exhibit D: Shareholder Returns Matter Most

Aon Hewitt studied engagement results for 1,500 companies and reported the following:[11]

» Where 60 percent to 70 percent of employees were engaged, average total shareholder return, or TSR, was 24.2 percent.

» In companies with only 49 percent to 60 percent of employees engaged, TSR fell to 9.1 percent.

> » And companies with 25 percent or fewer engaged employees reported a negative TSR.

Kenexa studied 64 organizations and found those in the top quartile for engagement achieved twice the annual net income of those in the bottom quartile.[12] It conducted another, longer-term study of 39 organizations, and those with engagement in the top quartile had seven times greater five-year TSR than organizations in the bottom quartile.[13]

Similarly, WorkUSA and Watson Wyatt surveyed 13,000 employees and found companies with highly engaged employees earn 26 percent more revenue per employee.[14] And there are dozens of similar studies I have omitted here that conclude the same thing, that high employee engagement drives all other important metrics.

C-Suite Executives Must Know This!

Our jury must completely grasp what these studies have in common: (a) each study found that engaged employees do more things better that substantially drive your CEO's primary metrics, and (b) each covered a broad range of industries and companies. Databases for the studies from Gallup and the Great Place to Work Institute cover millions of employees. Aon Hewitt drew conclusions from data that represent more than 1,500 companies. These rates eliminate potential queries from CEOs asking how do we know the same will be true for our companies. We all believe our companies have unique obstacles to engagement, the "you don't understand how things work here" mantra, and it is likely that CEOs from all of Aon Hewitt's 1,500 companies would have initially said the same. But the trend line for a total of 1,500 companies has proven that more engaged employees correlates with increases in shareholder returns *across all companies.*

Exhibit E: Getting to the All-In Costs of Turnover

What is your reaction when you hear an employee has decided to quit? Most of us would instinctively say, "It depends on who quits." The data above regarding engagement make clear that some employees are more valuable than others because they perform better or bring rare skills. But in general we would rather keep all employees whom we genuinely rate good or better because recruiting, hiring, and training their replacements is such a time-consuming and expensive hassle. And post hassle we risk getting a better employee or a worse one.

Several studies are available in the macro, from 30,000 feet, about the cost of turnover. These include:

» The Saratoga Institute observed that turnover costs organizations over 12 percent of pretax incomes, up to 40 percent for some.[15]

» In 2012 the Bureau of National Affairs estimated that U.S. businesses lose $11 billion each year due to turnover.[16]

» Kenexa reported turnover across the U.S. cost $25 billion annually just to train replacements.[17]

Although these results give us massive numbers that imply turnover is costly, they provide little convincing power for our C-suite jury. Another batch of studies has produced easy-to-use formulas that connect the cost of losing an employee to 100 percent of that employee's annual pay or a similar percentage.

I suspect that if your CEO read a report that said losing an employee costs 100 percent of that employee's annual pay, he or she would immediately move onto something more interesting, something more relevant about productivity or cost. The macro data provided above and the simplistic "1-times-something" formulas just do not convince. They will never drive a passion to improve retention on their own. They do not pass the "it has to be about our company or industry" test.

Our company, C-Suite Analytics, helps organizations place dollar values on turnover, and below are five actual turnover costs for five different jobs. Most importantly, CFOs have endorsed these studies for their organizations, which brings needed credibility for the right retention actions:[18]

» Health Partners of Western Ohio determined the cost of losing one physician was $225,808, which drove increased retention efforts.

» Bluegreen Corporation found the cost for losing one senior vacation specialist was $29,447. This cost was driven up by the average of 55 workdays to replace each leaving employee with a qualified replacement and then a strenuous learning curve of several months before that new hire could perform effectively on the phone.

» The VNA Hospice & Palliative Care of Southern California is a nonprofit agency that provides home health care and hospice services. Its cost to replace one registered nurse is $141,180. The main drivers of this cost were the number of days to fill openings and then the ramp-up time for new hires to learn the intricacies of their roles.

» A fast-growing software company found losing one software engineer cost $131,000. The CEO remarked that employee turnover was now seen as *the* critical metric for whether the organization reached its profitability goals.

» Schneider, a leader in logistics and transportation services, found losing a loader/unloader who works with its trucks cost the company $4,955. The notable discovery here is that we often think less-skilled employees can be easily replaced with few costs for recruiting, training, and lost productivity—the "just get another one" syndrome. Losing 100 loaders/unloaders would cost this company nearly one-half million dollars.

Turnover on the Rise

The U.S. Bureau of Labor Statistics (BLS) provides clear data from which we can predict who is at most risk for leaving their jobs. This is a far more reliable source than popular surveys that ask employees their future intentions regarding whether they will stay and why they will potentially quit. Let's look first at "quits" data, which represent the percentage of workers who are deciding to voluntarily quit their jobs (see Figure 1.2)

Figure 1.2. Voluntary Quits, 2009 through 2014 (%)

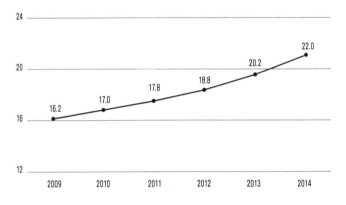

Source: Compiled from U.S. Bureau of Labor Statistics data (total nonfarm, seasonally adjusted).

These "quits" do not include employees fired or laid off, just those who leave on their own.

First we should note that unemployment is historically tiered by education, as in the more education one has, the better chance one has to find a job. This was true during the Great Recession as well as during the post-recession recovery period. As I write, U.S. unemployment for anyone with a four-year college degree is only 2.7 percent, whereas unemployment for those who fail to finish high school is a substantially higher 9.4 percent. Unemployment for high school grads is in between at 6.0 percent. All data reflect those who are age 25 and older.[19]

This is bad news for employers that hire professional, college-trained workers. But even among college-degreed workers who have jobs, many are underemployed, not working their dream jobs, and are therefore potentially available for upgrades from competing employers.

Most Costly Areas for Turnover No. 1: STEM Jobs

"Knowledge workers" is a term introduced about a decade ago to define employees who had advanced and oftentimes technical knowledge that was required to perform certain jobs. Since then the combination of our society's amped-up technology needs, the permanent low-skilled job eliminations from the recession, and the offshoring of more simple jobs has contributed to science, technology, engineering, and math (STEM) jobs representing a higher portion of our total openings. Every company needs some of these workers, and some industries require high percentages of them.

Various reports indicate that 3 million or more jobs have been unfilled for months because too few U.S. workers have the skills to fill them. Microsoft has contended that 120,000 new jobs in the United States will require a bachelor's degree in computer science but that the total number of graduates with this degree from all the nation's universities is just 40,000, and Microsoft predicted similar numbers throughout the remainder of this decade.[21]

Another report indicated "employment in STEM occupations will grow almost two times faster than the average for all occupations:[22]

- All Occupations: 10 percent
- All STEM Occupations: 19 percent
- Life Scientists: 27 percent
- Computer and Mathematical: 22 percent
- Physical Scientists: 15 percent
- Engineers: 11 percent

Compounding this challenge, our competitive advantage is at risk because other countries produce many more STEM graduates. In China, more than 40 percent of all degrees awarded are STEM degrees versus just 13 percent in the United States.[23]

The result of STEM shortages is that talent is more likely to be poached, replacement talent will take longer to find, replacement talent might be less effective, and technology projects will be slowed beyond deadlines. Perhaps the first step companies should take to recruit and retain STEM talent is to comprehensively calculate the cost of losing this talent when major projects and contracts are at stake. Doing so would increase all creative thinking for recruiting, and more importantly retaining, these literally precious employees.

STEM Talent Shortages Hit Our Wallets

The STEM talent shortage is reflected by how much we are paying college graduates with STEM-related degrees. The National Association of Colleges and Employers released starting salaries for the top bachelor's degree majors.[24] Here are the top 10 and their starting salaries when considering all undergraduate majors:

1. Petroleum Engineering, $95,300
2. Computer Science, $67,300
3. Aerospace/Aeronautical/Astronautical Engineering, $67,000
4. Computer Engineering, $66,600
5. Chemical Engineering, $66,000
6. Mechanical Engineering, $63,100
7. Engineering Technology, $63,000
8. Electrical/Electronics and Communications Engineering, $62,300
9. Management Information Systems/Business, $62,100
10. Civil Engineering, $62,100

Most Costly Areas for Turnover No. 2: Health Care

The aging of Americans, the onset of more complex treatments, and the Patient Protection and Affordable Care Act (PPACA) all point to the need for more qualified health care workers. Health care brings with it one other challenge: Its professional workers must be licensed, which limits the present and future applicant pool. No budding star can be promoted to a job or to duties that are beyond the license boundary, so those stars must instead go to school for years and then pass licensing exams.

For hospital CEOs, doctors have the greatest impact on revenue because most patients choose hospitals based on their doctors' affiliations. The return on investment (ROI) for hospitals is largely based on each doctor's specialty. On the high side, orthopedic surgeons generate an average of $2.7 million in revenue each year for their affiliated hospitals, invasive cardiologists $2.2 million, general surgeons $1.9 million, and neurosurgeons $1.7 million. Primary care physicians have moved up on the list and are now earning $1.6 million per year for their hospitals, and in fact now generate more revenue than the average specialty physician.[25]

What, then, is the price for a hospital to lose one or more physicians to a competing hospital in the same town?

Doctor shortages make turnover more expensive too. Reports indicate the United States is short 20,000 doctors today, and this number could quintuple over the next decade due to the aging of our people and our doctors.[26]

Doctor shortages and turnover are a strong threat to hospitals' revenues, but the turnover of nurses represents an equally strong threat to the quality of patient service.

BLS projections indicated that registered nurses will be the top job-growth occupation through 2020 as the number of employed nurses will grow by 26 percent. The projections also told of the need for half a million replacements in the nursing workforce, bringing the total number of job openings for nurses due to growth and replacements to 1.2 million by 2022.[27]

Making matters worse, would-be nurses cannot get trained. Nursing schools in the U.S. turned away more than 75,000 qualified applicants from baccalaureate and graduate nursing programs in 2011 due to insufficient numbers of faculty, clinical sites, classroom space, clinical preceptors, and budget constraints.[28] Over 62 percent of the nursing schools point to faculty shortages as a reason for not accepting all qualified applicants into their programs.[29]

Other data imply that nursing jobs are poorly designed or that the profession is historically understaffed. Researchers of one study noted that nurses are the least satisfied of all hospital employees,[30] and other research indicated a turnover rate of 13 percent for newly licensed registered nurses, while 37 percent felt ready to change jobs.[31]

We have conducted many nurse turnover cost studies with clients, and the single biggest driver of turnover costs is the number of days required to find and hire qualified replacements. The cost for each exit has a broad range for this reason, from $30,000 to greater than $60,000. The deepening nurse shortage will cause these costs to rise.

More importantly, many studies have stated that nurse shortages lead to more patient infections and more patient deaths. Now that results from Hospital Consumer Assessment of Healthcare Providers and Systems (HCAHPS) patient surveys directly affect levels of Medicare reimbursements, hospital CEOs must keep a sharp eye on nurse turnover because it now directly influences revenues.

Most Costly Areas for Turnover No. 3: Manufacturing

First the good news, that manufacturing is slowly but surely making its way back to the United States. This is due to many factors, including U.S. plants have become vastly more productive, foreign wages continue to rise, the Japan earthquake and resulting tsunami were a wake-up call to CEOs regarding supply chain vulnerabilities, currency values have shifted, domestic natural gas makes building things here cheaper, and overall product integrity is better in the United States.[32] Companies already committed to onshoring more talent include Cummins, Harley Davidson, John Deere, GE, Caterpillar, and Master Lock.[33] Apple also announced it would return some production from China.[34] And Google recently opened a state-of-the-art plant in Fort Worth, Texas, to assemble Motorola smartphones.[35]

The bad news is that whereas "manufacturing" once implied low-skilled jobs for shade-tree mechanics, modern-day factory jobs require training and oftentimes technical skills. And there is reason to believe that manufacturing's U.S. resurgence is being held back by shortages of talent.

Deloitte conducted a survey of executives for the National Association of Manufacturers and learned the following:[36]

- » Approximately 600,000 manufacturing jobs remain unfilled.
- » A total of 67 percent of respondents report a moderate or serious shortage of skilled production workers.
- » Over 70 percent say the skills shortages have negatively affected their ability to expand.

Combining these data with other research by the U.S. Bureau of Economic Analysis, the National Association of Manufacturers estimated that filling these 600,000 positions would result in more than 400,000 additional jobs being created, plus an increase in the gross domestic product (GDP) of 1.03 percent. But these positive outcomes happen only if those 600,000 jobs can be filled.[37]

It gets worse. This same report asserted that if Baby Boomers continue to retire at current rates, the shortage of highly skilled manufacturing workers could grow to approximately 875,000 machinists, welders, industrial-machinery mechanics, and industry engineers by 2020.[38] The BLS supported this finding as the median age of manufacturing workers is in the mid-40s and the average age of "high-skilled workers" is 56.[39] A third study by the Society of Manufacturing Engineers (now SME) resulted in a similar finding, indicating that the United States is facing a shortfall of 3 million factory workers.[40]

Non-STEM Jobs That Are Hard To Fill: Is It Quantity or Quality?

What do truck drivers,[41] bus drivers,[42] fireworks technicians,[43] and construction workers[44] have in common? All represent non-STEM jobs in which worker shortages have recently appeared in the news.

Given our current unemployment rate and the low skill levels for some available jobs, one wonders if these shortages are more about worker quality than quantity. The results from the first-ever international comparison of labor forces of 24 nations were unfavorable.[45] In that study the U.S. placed below international averages for basic problem-solving, reading, and math, with gaps between the more and less educated employees in the U.S. larger than those in many other countries. Younger U.S. workers lagged in almost every category.

No tests will tell us, though, how many or few members of our workforce will consistently show up and do so on time, work well with others, and take feedback constructively. And these are required skills for every job.

Your Closing Argument

Ladies and gentlemen of our C-suite jury, I have presented evidence throughout this proceeding that proves beyond a reasonable doubt the potentially extreme numbers of dollars you are leaving on the table regarding the engagement and retention levels of your employees. I ask you, therefore, to declare that these metrics merit top-5 status in your organizations.

Let me close this discussion by returning to the beginning, to that global engineering firm that might have your top technicians already penciled in on its organization charts for departure within the next five years.

The tool that gives these companies the ability to poach at incredibly higher levels is LinkedIn. After struggling with profitability for years, LinkedIn introduced its "Recruiter" tool that according to *Forbes* magazine is "turning the company's 161 million member profiles into the 21st-century version of a 'little black book.'"[46] Recruiter enables users to search this vast international database for keywords and make direct contact with individuals they target. The result is that LinkedIn's stock has soared, and the company is now investing 33 percent of its revenue in sales and marketing to sell more Recruiter seats.[47] In 2012, Adobe, for example, leased 70 Recruiter seats.[48] Accenture has abandoned outside search firms and directs its in-house recruiters to exclusively use LinkedIn.[49] Companies renew at 95 percent each year because the tool is addictive.[50]

Who needs traditional, external headhunters? Publicly traded recruiting companies such as Heidrick & Struggles and Monster Worldwide have seen stocks plummet by more than half.[51]

A full 98 percent of internal and external recruiters rely on LinkedIn to surface candidates for ultimate hire.[52] Importantly, these candidates do not need give any indication of interest to move but instead must only post their profiles. And LinkedIn is adding two new users every second.[53]

The fact is that stealing talent just got really cheap, and it has never been easier for your talent to apply. All employees must do is (1) post a LinkedIn profile, (2) include the most attractive keywords for their industries, and (3) respond to your competitors' inquiries via their keyboards—which you have paid for.

So let me recommend that after your CEOs search for that first number each morning for sales, quality, census, or production, you urge them to immediately ask this follow-up question: What must I do today to ensure I have the talent I need to improve this number tomorrow, next week, and next year?

5 Questions/Suggestions for You and Your C-Suite Executives to Overcome HR's Greatest Challenge

1. Ask yourself which of the following you have spent more time doing since the global economy plummeted in 2008: (1) reducing employee-related costs or (2) improving engagement and retention? Begin by making a list of your company's cost-cutting activities during this period that might include layoffs and other ways to cut staff, reducing or eliminating your pension plan, offshoring work to other countries, reducing pay, increasing workloads due to fewer staff, or cutting part-time hours to avoid additional health care costs due to the Affordable Care Act.

All these activities provide cuts in expenses and also risk additional disengagement and turnover. Given the data in this chapter regarding the lost dollars on the table due to disengagement and turnover, consider your potential dollar value for improving how hard your employees work and how long they stay, and whether this potential amount equals or exceeds the expenses you have saved.

NOTES: _____

_____

_____

_____

_____

2. How can you connect the dollar lessons in this chapter to currency values that will most motivate your CEO to change? One executive I know compared the cost of losing a call center rep to purchasing new equipment worth $12,000. In another company the chief HR officer compared the cost of losing one driver to the similar cost of losing one truck.

Steve Jobs opened his employees' and clients' eyes to new products with smart visuals such as sliding a new Mac into an interoffice envelope to show its slim size. What comparisons can you make that hit home?

NOTES: _____

_____

_____

_____

_____

3. Based on the data here and your own experience, which three jobs in your organization represent your greatest challenge for retention given the shortage of talent for them? Ask your C-suite to estimate the cost for losing one of these employees.

NOTES: _____

_____

_____

_____

_____

4. Identify a job or department that stands out as having a major impact on profitability but yet has a clearly seen shortage of engaged employees. Ask your C-suite to estimate the dollar value of this shortcoming.

NOTES: _____

_____

_____

_____

_____

5. Share key data about LinkedIn's surge to replace traditional search firms, and ask your C-suite executives in which departments or which jobs they most fear losing talent because they are likely receiving the most recruiting calls.

NOTES: _____

_____

_____

_____

_____

Chapter 2.

Two Broken Models:
Why Engagement Surveys
and Exit Surveys Fail

Now that we have connected employee engagement and retention to their high dollar values, let's study engagement surveys and exit surveys, which are two of the primary tools we use to launch our solutions. For starters we will study three figures, the data behind them, and then draw some fair conclusions: 26 percent, 31 percent, and $1.53 billion.

Since 2000, Gallup has surveyed a sample of U.S. workers each year to learn how engaged they are in their jobs.[1] Figure 2.1 shows the results.

Note that only the section on the left represents employees who are engaged in their jobs, as the middle section is labeled "not engaged" and the right section is labeled "actively disengaged." Gallup officially defined these groups as:[2]

> *Engaged employees* work with passion and feel a profound connection to their company. They drive innovation and move the organization forward.

Figure 2.1 Employee Engagement Among U.S. Working Population

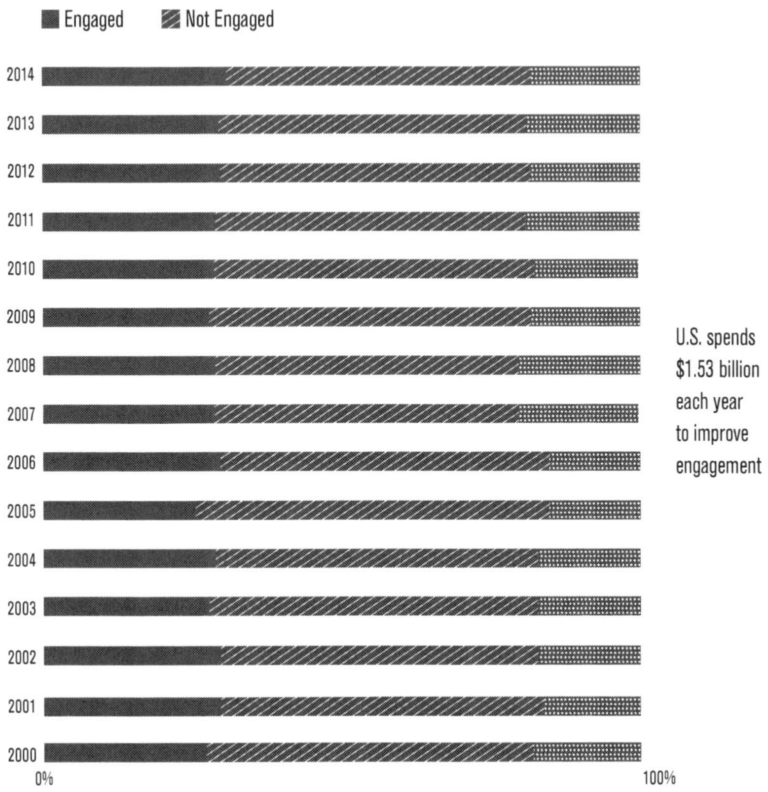

Adapted from Gallup Inc. published data. Copyright ©2014 Gallup Inc. All rights reserved. The content used with permission; however Gallup retains all rights of republication.

Not engaged employees are essentially checked out. They're sleepwalking through their workday putting time—but not energy or passion—into their work.

Actively disengaged employees aren't just unhappy at work; they're busy acting out their unhappiness. Every day, these workers undermine what their engaged coworkers accomplish.

Gallup reported that at most only 31 percent of our employees across the U.S. are engaged in their jobs. More importantly, throughout the past 15 years this percentage has hardly budged as the range for engaged employees is a tiny 26 percent to 31 percent, and there has been no pattern of progression. Or said another way, nothing we have done has had much impact on employee engagement. We are stuck.

For purposes of fair comparison, let's refer to the far-left data in Figure 2.1 as "top box," a term usually applied to consumer data that represents the percentage of consumers who rate your company with the highest possible score. Your organization might subscribe to an employee survey that also denotes the far left group as "engaged" and the middle group as "somewhat engaged" or another term that denotes a lesser but still positive level of engagement. For this discussion, let's limit our attention to the percentage of employees in the Gallup data in the far left group ("Engaged") and your own related survey results.

Many survey companies emphasize the combined percentages of the top and middle groups, perhaps to present higher percentages of data that appear to be more positive than only the top-box score. But the data presented in Chapter 1 make clear that employees whose engagement merits top-box status produce far more work than employees who score in the middle box. Objectively, it is more productive and more ambitious to direct our attention to those who are most engaged rather than to include the top and middle groups, which often *results* in a combined percentage of those who are not disengaged, although Gallup made clear that its middle group is disengaged.

Usually when I read reports on engagement trends, the authors often connect the resulting data to an outside, noncontrollable source such as the economy, unemployment, or the consumer confidence index. But media reports throughout these years indicate the U.S. has had strong *and* weak economies, high *and* low unemployment, and robust *and* lethargic consumer confidence scores, along with war, peace, and Democratic and Republican administrations.

The data make clear that our major external life forces have been highly inconsistent, whereas employee engagement has remained nearly the same. Or as the Gallup report stated, "While the state of the U.S. economy has changed substantially since 2000, the state of the American workplace has not."[3] A reasonable conclusion, then, is that economic and political conditions have little to do with employee engagement. So our collective inabilities to engage our workforces more fully are not being caused by circumstances outside of our organizations, but these shortcomings instead are being triggered by things we are doing or are not doing inside the buildings in which we work.

Let's also not overlook that the top-box range of 26 percent to 31 percent represents a frighteningly low number of engaged employees, especially when Gallup called the remaining 70 percent either "not engaged" or "actively disengaged." Yet this U.S.-only figure that tops out at 31 percent looks exemplary compared to three global studies that placed the percentage of engaged employees across the world at 19 percent, 17 percent, and just 11 percent.[4]

The High Cost of Low Engagement

Bersin reported[5] that companies spend a full $720 million annually to improve employee engagement. It said a little less than half this money, $325 million, is spent on vendors outside these companies with the rest being spent internally. This spending is likely to increase, though, as half the organizations Bersin surveyed have interest in spending more. This represents, Bersin said, a "fast-growing $1.53 billion market."[6]

On the one hand, this is another dollar amount that seems too large to comprehend. But on the other hand, most people who attend HR-related conferences and visit vendor exhibits see booth signs that advertise a multitude of employee engagement solutions. Vendors proclaim to improve engagement through better recruiting, hiring, onboarding, training, pay, benefits, coaching, surveys, career plans, recognition, policies, or improved communications.

Who is spending this money? Kenexa estimated that nearly 75 percent of companies with more than 10,000 employees conduct engagement surveys, and even 31 percent of those with 100 employees or less do so.[7] PWC believes 80 percent to 90 percent of large companies buy engagement surveys directly off the shelves of vendors.[8] Recalling that the $720 million mentioned earlier includes the dollars companies are spending in-house to fix engagement, it is fair to assume that nearly every significantly sized company is pitching in and either buying surveys and products or spending in-house resources for what they believe will become solutions.

These figures underscore that being stuck with no more than 31 percent of employees being engaged is not due to neglect. Most companies are actively surveying and "solving" engagement but without success.

We learned in Chapter 1 that employee engagement has massive impact on your company's profitability. And now we know we are spending hundreds of millions of dollars—and soon more than one billion dollars—and there is little if any return on investment (ROI) for this expenditure. This is akin to our society pumping extreme resources into improving cancer, crime, teenage smoking, or other universal worries with zero improvement. The truth is we are likely doing a better job on each of those challenges than we are with employee engagement. If our government were spending this money for no improvement, we would have to watch reports on it for a week on 24-hour news channels with panel debates about who is to blame.

When fully considering (a) that engagement levels have flatlined in the U.S. and are worse around the world, (b) that companies are spending many millions of dollars internally and externally to fix engagement, and (c) that companies are eager to spend even more money on likely the same solutions, this combination of data says to me:

1. That we have a problem and we do not know how to fix it, that all of the surveying we have done, action plans we

have developed, and the solutions we have bought have on average not moved the needle.

2. That instead of looking externally for either excuses or solutions, we need to look inside our companies and have the courage to address the real issues.

3. That if only 31 percent or fewer of your companies' employees score in the top box, your CEO is irresponsible for not demanding better solutions; succeeding just 30 percent of the time is only OK in baseball.

Here's one hint for an effective solution. I often ask groups of CEOs and other executives to raise their hands if they can think of at least one key manager in their organizations who cannot build trust with their teams. Every time I have asked this question, nearly all in the room have raised their hands. Why, then, do they continue to survey these managers' employees if they already know the results they will get and also the root of the problem?

Out with the Old

Have you ever heard a manager say he or she would not hire someone from a competitor because that person has been "trained wrong?" That the manager would rather start fresh with someone he or she could train from the start with no experience at all?

This always seems like an extreme position to me. Surely there is some good that can be transferred from an old way of thinking to a new way of thinking, no matter how different those approaches, roles, or skills might be.

But let me suggest that the current ways companies manage retention and engagement is so far off course that much if not all of the old must go. Let's look at 12 common beliefs regarding exit surveys and engagement surveys and the truth about each (see Table 2.1). You can then decide whether to spackle the holes in the wall or just to tear down the wall.

Table 2.1. Exit Surveys and Engagement Surveys

Topic	Belief	Truth
Exit Surveys	Exiting employees tell true reasons for leaving	In the book *The Truth about Lies in the Workplace*, telling the truth during exit surveys is career suicide.*
	HR distributes reports of leading exit reasons, and executives take action	Little action happens based on these reports
	HR steadfastly believes exit surveys help	I've asked 6,000 HR executives if exit surveys have significantly helped their companies and received yes responses from just 12
Engagement Surveys	Employees must hide behind anonymity to tell us the truth	Anonymity says we assume you distrust us, and it also blocks us from segmenting the opinions of top performers
	Surveys provide benchmarks for how our engagement levels compare to peer companies	Learning how close your company is to average provides a false sense of achievement; if your top-box score is 30 percent and the benchmark is 29, should you feel good that 70 percent of your employees are less than fully engaged?
	Surveys tell us what our employees most want us to improve	Surveys tell opinions but not importance, so items with lowest scores might not matter as much to employees as other items with higher scores
	Leaders and HR assume one-size-fits-all programs lead to improved engagement	Employees are like snowflakes, and they stay and become engaged for things they get uniquely from you
	Managers submit action plans that will improve engagement	Managers and their executives make a nonintuitive link that employees want programs versus better supervision, so action plans contain suggestion boxes, town hall meetings, and employee-of-the-month awards, all of which do not improve supervision
	Managers keep all commitments and fulfill their action plans	Companies set standards and track managers' performances against critical metrics; what tracking mechanism do you have in place for managers' engagement survey action plans?
	Surveying employees once per year gives a good measure of employee engagement	Would you solicit feedback from your best customers just once per year?
	Leaders with substandard scores are held accountable for improvement	With no interim measures, that leader's team might suffer through another year of low engagement before progress is reassessed
	Leaders with repeated substandard scores are removed from their positions	Measure this within your own company; how often have leaders been fired or moved out of leadership roles because of repeated low engagement survey results?

* Carol Kinsey Goman, *The Truth about Lies in the Workplace: How to Spot Liars and What to Do About Them* (San Francisco: Berrett-Koehler, 2013).

Are Exit Surveys a Bad Habit?

From the treetops, exit surveys should bring gold for developing the right employee retention solutions. The belief is that employees who leave will tell us why, and we can then fix the problems. Reality, though, tells a different tale.

For a variety of reasons, once employees say "I quit," their overall credibility in the exit interview is diminished. Add this to the following list of why exit surveys come up short:

> » Most surveys are too long; all we want is for employees to tell us why they are quitting rather than to score pay, benefits, and the cafeteria on a scale of 1 to 10; survey length also contributes to low response rates on automated surveys.
> » We readily accept a verbal or checked response of "better opportunity," which gives us no clue how we can improve; the right follow-up questions are, "Why did you look?" and "What more could we have done to keep you?"
> » We promise to keep the exit information confidential, which ties our hands to address any problem.
> » We circulate summary reports with no specific, achievable recommendations for action or names of people who will be accountable for implementation.

Most importantly, employees hold back on telling the truth. In Carol Kinsey Goman's book *The Truth about Lies in the Workplace*, she advised those who leave, "Don't burn bridges. Say you're leaving for personal growth. Telling the truth here can be career suicide."[9]

Exit interviews are autopsies but not as scientific. The employee is gone, and the only benefit is to learn a tip or two to retain other employees. Recording that someone left due to low pay does not usually result in others getting a raise or in soul-searching to learn which remaining employees should be targeted for more money or more responsibility. And accepting "attendance" or "tardiness" as reasons for leaving rarely leads to solving why you hired employees who miss too much work or show up late. Or why you failed to engage them.

As my friend and HRsoft CEO David Kennedy once said, "Exit surveys are the perfect combination of extensive activity with absolutely no positive result."[10]

When speaking to HR groups over the past two years, I have asked first how many conduct exit surveys for their organizations and then, immediately after, how many have significantly improved their organizations as a result. So far about 6,000 HR professionals have said yes to the first question, and 12 have said yes to the second question. Mathematically, this places the yes respondent percentage at 0.002. If we stretch our thinking to assume that for every yes there were 10 others in the room who wanted to say yes but held back, the percentage of positive responses would still be just 2 percent.

This poll represents the common trend that organizations invest time and money into exit surveys year after year and gain little or nothing for it. Yet HR executives continue to reflexively conduct exit surveys—maybe because they have always done them, or because other companies do them, or because vendors send them benchmark data that they think is valuable. Or perhaps they think they will eventually uncover an example of sexual harassment or another form of abuse that makes all this activity worthwhile. A good metaphor for conducting exit surveys is sliding our tongue over a recently chipped tooth. We cannot resist doing it even though we know it won't fix the tooth.

The only reason to continue conducting exit surveys is if you repeatedly apply the resulting data to make your company better. None of the four choices above appear to do so. I will offer a better way to conduct exit surveys in Chapter 8.

The Ineffective Nooks and Crannies
of Engagement Surveys

Engagement surveys offer a similar logical path to improvement. We ask employees about critical issues, they tell us what works and what does not work, and we make every reasonable effort to solve the problems. The holes in this process are the following:

» Each employee's opinion is considered to be equal when his or her contributions to productivity are not.

» Managers respond with the assumption that the collective opinions and interests of their individual team members can be reduced to one set of data, as if their employees have identical opinions.

» Each survey item is treated equally, so we presume the lowest score should garner the most attention.

» Benchmarks provide false security, as we are pleased to score one point better than average when average means mediocre; would your CEO be pleased if sales were one hair better than mediocre?

» Leaders are rarely held accountable for making sustained improvements that raise future scores.

» The bridge from results to solutions is believed to be short and intuitive, as surely it is easy to fix most of the identified problems.

A Global Engagement Survey Vendor's Instructions

Let's look more closely into this "bridge from results to solutions." I recently asked an executive with a global HR consulting company if his engagement survey division's role was to help its client organizations improve engagement or just provide data. He consulted with a peer executive and wrote back the following: *"They don't generally get involved in the actions taken by an org in response to the engagement results—really just delivery of the survey and then reporting."*[11]

This quote is reinforced by a story told to us by the HR executive of an urban hospital. He had used a different global survey company than the one quoted above to conduct an engagement survey when we first met. This hospital had just received survey results that showed it had moved backward, and its executives were seeking fast help to reverse this course.

As we dug through the data, we found the survey company's directives to managers for the lowest-scoring units. Here are those directives, verbatim:

>> A visible/approachable manager.
>> A commitment to the patient experience.
>> Adequate materials/equipment.
>> A sense of camaraderie on the team.

That is it. No tactics, not even specific instructions for either a program or for supervisory solutions. Just make it happen.

How could these instructions possibly help these managers succeed?

More importantly, these tales drive home a crucial truth about both engagement and exit surveys that must re-direct our thinking: *They provide data but they do not provide solutions.*

Holding Managers Accountable for
Employee Survey Results

How many times in a month do you receive an e-mail from a company whose services you have recently used, asking you to rate that service? Or a phone call to do the same? Every time I take my Acura into the shop, this scenario occurs:

» I am asked to complete a survey before I leave.
» Then I am asked at the end of the survey if I rated any item less than perfect, so they can fix that item on the spot.
» Then I am called a day later by the service manager to elicit more feedback.
» And I am also called after that by Acura headquarters to get even more feedback.

With examples like this, you might say that companies survey you far too often.

But let's flip the survey discussion to the perspective of marketing directors. Companies survey customers constantly because they want your repeat business. Companies survey customers when new products are introduced into the market, new locations are opened, new managers are put into customer-service leadership roles, when competitors introduce competing products, and for other reasons too many to mention. And when data indicate substandard performance, areas for improvement are expeditiously addressed. This is because customers are the lifeline of any business. Companies must be obsessed with their customers to stay in business.

So ask yourself if your employees matter to your company as much as your customers. Or if you work in health care, whether your employees matter as much as your patients. We have all been weaned on the mantras of "Please employees first and then you'll please your customers," or "We can't satisfy our customers if we don't satisfy our employees first." But, really, do our actions support that our employees are held on the same level as our customers?

One way to face this question squarely is to compare your processes for customer surveys and employee surveys. Table 2.2 presents a few questions to consider.

Table 2.2. Survey Practices for Employees vs. Customers

Question	Customers	Employees
1. How often do you survey your customers and your employees?		
2. Which events trigger a customer survey and an employee survey?		
3. Do you schedule customer and employee surveys during normal times or at times when you will achieve optimal results?		
4. How many days does it take for your company to implement changes when survey results require improvement?		
5. When improvement is required, how many days into the future do you resurvey?		
6. Do real consequences happen for managers whose departments need significant improvement based on survey results that directly affect their performance ratings, pay, and promotional opportunities?		
7. How many managers have you terminated in the past year because they have failed to improve their survey results?		

We would all agree that processes for surveying customers and surveying employees might have some differences and still be effective. One example is it would be awkward to survey employees after each experience as you might do with your customers. And there is certainly a survey burnout factor whereby employees might have lower response rates if you surveyed them too often—especially if they saw no changes as a result.

But the questions that deserve most discussion from the questionnaire in Table 2.2 are numbers 6 and 7: "Do real consequences happen for managers whose departments need significant improvement based on survey results that directly affect their performance ratings, pay, and promotional opportunities?" and "How many managers have you terminated in the past year because they have failed to improve their survey results?" Recently we asked a sample of HR professionals this question: "Which of the following does your company do with managers who have consistently low employee survey results?" We received these results:

» We note it on their performance appraisals: 28 percent.
» Their bonus or compensation is directly impacted: 5 percent.
» We terminate them or put them in nonsupervisory roles: 5 percent.
» Nothing really happens: 63 percent.

Should we substitute "low customer survey results" rather than ask about employee survey results, we strongly suspect the outcomes would tilt toward harsher consequences for managers. In fact, the term "lip service" comes to mind when considering those phrases mentioned above that imply companies treat customers and employees the same.

What matters most here is how your company handles managers who consistently fail to score adequately on employee surveys and therefore fail to engage their teams. Do these managers face meaningful consequences that ensure they either improve quickly or leave the company? Or do they carry on as though the survey results drive no real consequences?

Absence of management accountability continues regarding unwanted turnover, too. We partnered with ExecuNet to survey CEOs on whether they are held accountable for retaining their executives in their organizations and here is the percent of respondents for each category of accountability:[12]

» It hurts our company's productivity: 39 percent.
» The rest of my management team is disappointed: 27 percent.
» I feel I've let the shareholders down: 18 percent.
» There is no accountability: 9 percent.
» My pay or bonus is directly reduced: 4 percent.

» Other: 3 percent.

These results say more about contrition than about accountability. When we asked these same CEOs if they tie their direct reports' employee retention outcomes to compensation, 18 percent said yes, 78 percent said no, and the remaining 4 percent did not know. The report stated these conclusions:

» Simply put, most executives face no meaningful financial consequences if they fail to retain their top performers.

» The lack of accountability among CEOs for retaining their best direct reports also has a trickle-down effect in lower levels of management. The apparent approach: Let HR deal with it later.

Thinking back to how we manage customers versus employees, ask yourself this: Would you direct a manager who is in charge of a highly profitable but dissatisfied set of customers to create an action plan to improve customer service and then check in with those customers one year later to see if that plan worked? Or would you handle patient concerns this way in a hospital?

The important question to ask regarding your employee survey is, does it make your organization better? Have you found ways to address the obstacles described in this section, so your survey contributes real value, or do you conduct an employee survey only because it is a trend, that other companies conduct them, too? For some organizations, employee survey time resembles budget time as in "Already? Do we have to do that survey again so soon?," especially if a recent event causes executives to think survey scores will dip as a result. And in their worst case, engagement surveys lead to thick, time-consuming, everyone-gets-sucked-into-the-vortex kind of activities. Those organizations should dig deeply to improve their survey outcomes or invest their time and money elsewhere.

Let's revisit our three numbers from the beginning of this chapter. Since 2000 the percentage of U.S. employees who are engaged in their jobs has peaked at 31 percent with a low reading of 26 percent, so the number of engaged employees is low, and it is not improving. And we are on the verge of spending $1.53 billion each year on solutions that have proven across the board to be wrong.

5 Questions/Suggestions for You and Your C-Suite Executives to Overcome HR's Greatest Challenge

1. After teaching your C-suite executives the productivity impact of those who score in the top box of engagement surveys, ask them if they'd like to see benchmark results of your percentage of top-box employees versus competitor companies. Your survey company can likely show you the percentage of top-box scorers for each department, too. If your executives say yes, ask your survey company to provide this information.

NOTES: _____

_____

_____

_____

_____

2. Ask your C-suite executives if they can identify one way your company or their departments have improved from exit survey results.

NOTES: _____

_____

_____

_____

_____

3. Complete Table 2.2 that compares survey methods for customers and employees and share it with your C-suite executives. Ask your

C-suite executives if they think your analysis is correct and also if they believe your current methods drive the best chance to improve engagement.

NOTES: _____

_____

_____

_____

_____

4. If you can access these data, study managers' engagement survey scores for the last three administrations to learn which ones scored consistently high and low. Then ask your C-suite to guess which managers scored that way.

NOTES: _____

_____

_____

_____

_____

5. Bring a sample of a manager survey action plan activities to your C-suite executives and ask them (a) if they know if these plans have been carried out and (b) if they believe these activities will make a difference.

NOTES: _____

_____

_____

_____

_____

Part II: Solutions

Chapter 3.

Think Like Your CEO: Drive Engagement and Retention Like You Drive Sales and Service

Have you ever wondered how much your CEO believes you *personally* contribute to productivity, revenue, growth, and profitability? Not how well you do your job, how you compare with other HR executives, or how effectively you manage your team. Not how well you respond to others' needs or provide stout administrative services that keep the trains running on time. But where you stand compared to others on the executive team for making major contributions that are the difference between your company's success and failure.

Isn't this the defining question for whether we are awarded the oft-discussed "seat at the table?"

Some will say our roles limit us. We are not directly involved in sales or service or in making or shipping products. We are not directly involved in achieving the types of numbers the CFO announces in monthly updates to the executive team and the board.

We are, however, the engine that ensures the right people are placed in those sales and service jobs and that they perform their best. And we are the people who design the ways our companies manage about 70 percent of their total operating expenses.[1] The truth is that executive level HR professionals in most organizations have unlimited opportunities to influence productivity, revenue, growth, and profitability. We just have to figure out how.

The Metrus Group has done extensive work comparing executives' and managers' perceptions of their various support departments. Just how effective is HR? The survey results shown in Figure 3.1 represent the percentage of respondents who rated each department favorably and include responses from 35 different industries.

Figure 3.1 Ratings of Departmental Internal Customer Service, 2006

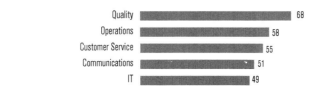

Source: Adapted from Jerry Seibert and John Lingle, "Internal Customer Service: Has It Improved?" Quality Progress, March 2007, http://www.metrus.com/resources/Internal_Customer_Service_Has_It_Improved.pdf.

Some would say thank goodness for marketing. Let's drill down much deeper, though, and find answers to what is holding us back.

The Economist Intelligence Unit conducted a global survey of C-level executives on how HR can play bigger role in driving growth.[2] More than half of the respondents were CEOs, and the survey was dominated by U.S. companies. The results are instructive for what our CEOs want us to be:

» "What is most likely to harm your organization financially over the next 12 months?" Insufficient talent: 53 percent.

» "What are the obstacles to HR taking a greater role in strategic planning?"

• Is too focused on processes and rules—not a "big

picture" person: 41 percent.
- Doesn't understand the business well enough: 36 percent.
- Is not of the same caliber as other C-suite executives: 29 percent.
- Behaves like an independent advisor and service provider rather than a fully invested member of the management team: 21 percent.
» "How involved is your head of HR in strategic planning versus how involved do you want him or her to be?"
- HR is a key player: 15 percent.
- Want HR to play key player role: 29 percent.

What does it tell us that our executives can readily describe why we come up short on strategic planning contributions, yet only 29 percent of them prefer that we get more involved? Maybe it is because of how they see our actual performance. Executives were asked to rate their top HR leaders on several key factors, and the percentage who scored their HR leaders as excellent for any one category peaked at 22:
» Understanding the HR needs of the business: 22 percent.
» Leading the HR function: 21 percent.
» Evaluating employee performance: 17 percent.
» Identifying and recruiting key talent: 16 percent.
» Managing benefit and compensation costs: 15 percent.

In fairness, these data present the same obstacle as engagement surveys: They describe a group of people as all being the same. Each HR executive is different, and these data might represent your executives' opinions of your work—or not.

One disadvantage we have is that very few CEOs have ever worked in HR versus some of those departments that are listed above HR in Figure 3.1. About one-third of *Fortune* 500 CEOs began their careers in finance, just over 20 percent in sales and marketing, and most of the rest in operations, engineering, legal, and consulting.[3]

CEOs are hired in part because they have learned how to manage people and recognize the importance of effective people-management processes. But this reason is far different from understanding first-hand the obstacles HR leaders face when gaining and maintaining credibility, managing an administratively tight ship, and other requirements of our jobs. This reason also implies CEOs might not know how to effectively use HR professionals based on their own career experiences. It becomes essential, then, that we find the answer to that question ourselves and then teach them.

Can HR Executives See the Engagement and Retention Pathway?

Connecting dots between (a) the huge financial impact of engagement and retention, (b) the costly and universal failure to improve engagement that also influences turnover, and (c) the not-so-flattering data in the previous section regarding executive-level HR professionals, one must ask this question: How can we lead our organizations to greatly improve these wannabe top-5 metrics?

A recent study of HR professionals reinforced how much we struggle with engagement and retention solutions. HR respondents rated their top five priorities, and these included improving engagement and retention. Then when asked to *rate their effectiveness* at each of these challenges, they ranked improving engagement and retention at the bottom.[4] They apparently lack the tools, support, or know-how to move these areas forward. This outcome squares with the "big investment, no progress" data we saw in Chapter 2. So let us shine light on the right path.

Exercise: Choose the Right P-Word

Several years ago one of the major global consulting firms asked me to train its executives on how to influence the managers beneath them. We met in three different cities around the world to accommodate this large international team. During each session, the first two days were used to learn other new concepts, and I was the trainer for day three.

The day one opening exercise caught me off guard when I heard it the first time. A facilitator asked the executives to tackle a question at their tables, map out their team response on flip charts, and then present that answer to the total group. The question was provocative and multiple choice: "If you are helping a client company improve productivity, where would you start? With products? With people? With processes?"

As a curious onlooker, I was oblivious to the lesson that was to come. With HR in my blood, it seemed likely the answer was "people" or maybe even "all of the above." Only when the facilitator announced the answer did I begin to learn the lesson.

The answer was "processes." The facilitator explained that a company's products were the result of the overall effectiveness of product development processes like customer focus groups, competitor analysis, and consumer behaviors. And that having the right people was dependent on hiring processes, leadership development, and other activities that composed the total set of people-management processes. Processes drive everything in organizations, he said. That lit the light.

As importantly, the facilitator explained, these processes must be consistently applied, "baked in" as some would say, and institutionalized as "the way we do things here, 100 percent of the time." Once the right processes have been identified, all must agree to do them the right way, every day.

Let's now introduce another p-word into this discussion: "programs." We will use programs as the umbrella word that includes recognition activities like employee of the month and employee appreciation week, communications programs like town hall meetings and newsletters, and career development programs such as brown-bag lunches with speakers. By the end of this chapter I hope to convince you that these programs do little to drive engagement and retention and that we must move from programs to the right processes to succeed.

So we are senior HR professionals in search of effective processes for engagement and retention. And here's the good news: Our CEOs and other executives have already defined these processes for us in the form of sales and service. Let's take the path they have chosen for their favorite, universally accepted top-level metrics and put it to work for us.

What Are Your Company's Processes to Drive Sales and Service?

We should all do this exercise, immediately in our current companies and in the future if we work somewhere else. Recalling Mark Jin's advice as noted in the Introduction, this exercise requires courage.

Begin by identifying who is responsible for designing the processes for both sales and service in your company. The sales process leader might be the top sales executive or top marketing executive, whereas you might find the service process leader in a department labeled "quality." Those who work for grant-funded nonprofit organizations would likely focus on quality only unless gaining other revenue is important to make ends meet.

Make an appointment to interview these two people, and ask the eight questions in Table 3.1.

Table 3.1 Sales and Services Process Interview Questions

1. What are the processes our company has in place, step by step, to make sales/service successful?

2. What data do you have that ensures these processes drive more revenue?

3. How do you measure whether our employees execute these processes?

4. How do you establish annual goals for sales/service?

5. Who is accountable for achieving these goals?

6. What are the consequences for employees who do these processes consistently and well?

7. What are the consequences for employees who fail to do these processes?

8. If you had to name just one process step as most important, what would it be?

Review your notes after these meetings and look for trends. You will likely find components of traditional sales and service process models that include (a) financial analysis to connect activities to revenue, (b) performance standards to measure achievement, (c) training and other tools for execution, (d) forecasting in some cases and especially for sales, and then (e) accountability for performance against standards.

Now we have our map, our pathway to move from programs to processes and from engagement and retention quicksand to success. Your CEO instinctively understands that these processes drive the bloodlines of your business and will soon embrace your fresh-thinking, process-based approach. For those of us who have spent years in executive meetings hearing about our companies' successes and challenges, these methods have been consistently streaming into our ears and our eyes by way of verbal and written reports. Or to add one more facial reference, they have been right under our collective noses.

5 Process Steps to Significantly Improve Engagement and Retention

Next up, let's compare the processes we learned for our companies' sales and service strategies with our processes for engagement and retention. Our theory will be that because sales and service are top-5 metrics, their processes have been honed into fine form. And because engagement and retention merit top-5 metric status but have so far failed to attain it, we will find the shortcomings in our processes for engagement and retention and fix them.

I will supply processes for sales and service based on my experience and do the same for commonly-used processes related to engagement and retention. You now know your company's sales and service processes from your interviews and your processes for engagement and retention, so feel free to replace my responses below with your own.

During your interviews you asked the questions in Table 3.1, which included, "What data do you have that ensures these processes drive more revenue?" Responses likely drew the correlations from successful process implementation to revenue with words such as "margins" for selling products or by key leaders knowing correlations for service improvements such as "for each 2 percent increase in this quality metric, we know we increase revenues by 4 percent." So let's name our first comparative process "Convert to Dollars" and begin building our comparative processes in Table 3.2.

Table 3.2. Continually-Building Engagement and Retention Processes Chart

Comparative Processes	Sales	Service
1. Convert to dollars	Margins: "This product brings a 22% margin, which results in $4,000 for each sale going right to the bottom line"	Correlations: "For each 2% improvement in our service score, our revenues increase by $124,000"

So if sales and service are top-5 metrics and if your CEO and other executives can readily translate their outcomes to dollars, would we increase their attention if we converted engagement and retention to dollars, too? Let's add a column for engagement and retention in Table 3.3.

Table 3.3. Continually-Building Engagement and Retention Processes Chart

Comparative Processes	Sales	Service	Engagement and Retention
1. Convert to dollars	Margins: "This product brings a 22% margin, which results in $4,000 for each sale going right to the bottom line"	Correlations: "For each 2% improvement in our service score, our revenues increase by $124,000"	

What belongs in the empty engagement and retention box? Some of you might have the types of correlative studies referenced in Chapter 1, but my decades-long experience tells me nearly all companies think of turnover as a percentage of employees who leave and engagement as scores on the most recent survey. Sometimes comparisons to benchmarks are included to anchor your data to similar companies. In other words, HR presents outcomes without reference to dollars, which is the language of CEOs, CFOs, and your C-suite colleagues as indicated now in Table 3.4.

Table 3.4. Continually-Building Engagement and Retention Processes Chart

Comparative Processes	Sales	Service	Engagement and Retention
1. Convert to dollars	Margins: "This product brings a 22% margin, which results in $4,000 for each sale going right to the bottom line"	Correlations: "For each 2% improvement in our service score, our revenues increase by $124,000"	Results reported in percentages and scores with no correlations to dollars; sometimes include comparisons to benchmarks

Ask yourself now if your executives respond to engagement and retention data with as much corrective energy as they do to sales and service data. If you answer no, then one solution is to translate engagement and retention data into the dollar-driven lexicon of those at the top. I will present ways to do this in Chapter 4.

The second process trend we identified is standards, or some would say "goals." During your interviews you asked as Question #3, "How do you measure whether our employees execute these processes?" Your process leaders likely said the surest measure is whether employees meet their sales and service goals.

Both sales and service are traditionally goal-driven strategies, and organizations establish these goals for the total company, for managers of sales and service teams, and for individual employees. Achieving sales goals drives revenue, and service goals are critical for increasing repeat sales and referrals as noted in Table 3.5.

Table 3.5. Continually-Building Engagement and Retention Processes Chart

Comparative Processes	Sales	Service	Engagement and Retention
1. Convert to dollars	Margins: "This product brings a 22% margin, which results in $4,000 for each sale going right to the bottom line"	Correlations: "For each 2% improvement in our service score, our revenues increase by $124,000"	Results reported in percentages and scores with no correlations to dollars; sometimes include comparisons to benchmarks
2. Establish goals	Essential for revenue generation and defined for total company, sales managers, and sales employees; goals are usually increased year to year and sometimes quarter to quarter	Drive additional business from current customers and referrals; defined for total company, service managers, and service employees	

Now let's address what types of goals organizations usually set for engagement and retention. My experience is that many organizations set retention goals for the total organization, but few establish retention goals below the organizational level. Engagement goals are far scarcer, and instead organizations aim to improve their survey scores over their most recent survey results and also ahead of comparative external benchmarks their survey providers might supply. These benchmarks might be tailored by industry or by company size as indicated in Table 3.6.

Table 3.6. Continually-Building Engagement and Retention Processes Chart

Comparative Processes	Sales	Service	Engagement and Retention
1. Convert to dollars	Margins: "This product brings a 22% margin, which results in $4,000 for each sale going right to the bottom line"	Correlations: "For each 2% improvement in our service score, our revenues increase by $124,000"	Results reported in percentages and scores with no correlations to dollars; sometimes include comparisons to benchmarks
2. Establish goals	Essential for revenue generation and defined for total company, sales managers, and sales employees; goals are increased year to year and sometimes quarter to quarter	Drive additional business from current customers and referrals; defined for total company, service managers, and service employees	Most times retention goals either are not set at all or are set for the total organization; engagement goals are rarely established, and past scores and benchmarks serve as standards without specific improvement objectives

Importantly, the absence of engagement goals makes the objective "do one notch better" than past scores and benchmarks. There are no considerations for correlations to profitability or any stretch goals. Just do better. The belief is that if we increase by one hair, we are trending up versus down, which is good. Chapter 5 is devoted to the best methods for establishing engagement and retention goals.

Let's now move to the third common process step—the "tools" part. During your interviews you asked as your first question, "What are the processes our company has in place, step by step, to make sales/service successful?" You likely heard many examples and were handed process flow charts, training curricula, collateral materials, sales and service scripts, and all other things that make up how your company manages the main parts of your business that keep you in business. The heart of these processes, though, is training and tools. So we will label this third process "train and provide tools" and enter some of the usual ones for sales and service in Table 3.7.

Table 3.7. Continually-Building Engagement and Retention Processes Chart

Comparative Processes	Sales	Service	Engagement and Retention
1. Convert to dollars	Margins: "This product brings a 22% margin, which results in $4,000 for each sale going right to the bottom line"	Correlations: "For each 2% improvement in our service score, our revenues increase by $124,000"	Results reported in percentages and scores with no correlations to dollars; sometimes include comparisons to benchmarks
2. Establish goals	Essential for revenue generation and defined for total company, sales managers, and sales employees; goals are increased year to year and sometimes quarter to quarter	Drive additional business from current customers and referrals; defined for total company, service managers, and service employees	Most times retention goals either are not set at all or are set for the total organization; engagement goals are rarely estab-lished, and past scores and benchmarks serve as standards without specific improvement objectives
3. Train and provide tools	Product training, sales training, collateral sales materials, administrative tools and training to use them	Product training, service training, administrative tools and training to use them	

What, then, are our training and tools for engagement and retention? Identifying these requires tapping into the vast pool of activities included in the $1.53 billion that will soon be spent on engagement alone as referenced in Chapter 2.[5] And this box also brings to mind one of those p-words: "programs."

Some organizations would place pay and benefits in the box labeled training and tools for engagement and retention, although studies tell us neither pay nor benefits usually make the top three reasons why employees stay or engage. Our list should surely include engagement surveys, exit surveys, and resulting reports and action plans. All types of management training and supervisory training should be included, as well as executive and management coaching.

Also include the plethora of employee programs like career fairs, employee appreciation week, and community walks to raise funds for charities. Include rewards like trips to Hawaii for top sales producers. And surveys indicate many companies use total compensation statements as a way to entice people to stay and work harder.

This list becomes "kitchen sink" for most companies, resulting in naming many activities and incentives you offer that supposedly affect employees' decisions to stay and give their best. I will write in a sample of the above but suggest you write in the top three things your company does that you believe contribute the most in Table 3.8.

Table 3.8. Continually-Building Engagement and Retention Processes Chart

Comparative Processes	Sales	Service	Engagement and Retention
1. Convert to dollars	Margins: "This product brings a 22% margin, which results in $4,000 for each sale going right to the bottom line"	Correlations: "For each 2% improvement in our service score, our revenues increase by $124,000"	Results reported in percentages and scores with no correlations to dollars; sometimes include comparisons to benchmarks
2. Establish goals	Essential for revenue generation and defined for total company, sales managers, and sales employees; goals are increased year to year and sometimes quarter to quarter	Drive additional business from current customers and referrals; defined for total company, service managers, and service employees	Most times retention goals either are not set at all or are set for the total organization; engagement goals are rarely established, and past scores and benchmarks serve as standards without specific improvement objectives
3. Train and provide tools	Product training, sales training, collateral sales materials, administrative tools and training to use them	Product training, service training, administrative tools and training to use them	Compensation, benefits, management and supervisory training, surveys, employee programs

In Chapter 6, I will recommend that you implement stay interviews as the absolutely most effective tools to improve engagement and retention.

Our fourth common process step is forecasting. Sales executives use forecasting to predict future sales, so they are alerted if goals might be missed or if resources must be reallocated to achieve them. Forecasting is also used for sales managers to coach salespeople when forecasts come up short. Salespeople are motivated by forecasts either to improve their pipelines or to close the predicted deals. Typical sales forecasts include timelines such as projected sales for the next month/quarter/year, projected revenues, and the likely percentage each sale will close. Projected revenue is then calculated with the following formula: projected revenues x likely percentage to close.

In the far bigger picture, CEOs use forecasts to make important disclosures to stock analysts and their boards regarding future earnings. Careers sometimes rest on the accuracy of these forecasts.

Forecasts are less common regarding service because the expectation is that service standards will always be achieved or exceeded. Unless noted obstacles must be removed before standards can be achieved, the standard is the forecast.

So let's enter forecasting into our comparative process grid by labeling it "Forecast Future Performance" and include summary comments for sales and service in Table 3.9.

Table 3.9. Continually-Building Engagement and Retention Processes Chart

Comparative Processes	Sales	Service	Engagement and Retention
1. Convert to dollars	Margins: "This product brings a 22% margin, which results in $4,000 for each sale going right to the bottom line"	Correlations: "For each 2% improvement in our service score, our revenues increase by $124,000"	Results reported in percentages and scores with no correlations to dollars; sometimes include comparisons to benchmarks
2. Establish goals	Essential for revenue generation and defined for total company, sales managers, and sales employees; goals are increased year to year and sometimes quarter to quarter	Drive additional business from current customers and referrals; defined for total company, service managers, and service employees	Most times retention goals either are not set at all or are set for the total organization; engagement goals are rarely established, and past scores and benchmarks serve as standards without specific improvement objectives
3. Train and provide tools	Product training, sales training, collateral sales materials, administrative tools and training to use them	Product training, service training, administrative tools and training to use them	Compensation, benefits, management and supervisory training, surveys, employee programs
4. Forecast future performance	Sales executives use forecasts to reallocate resources and sometimes alert CEOs; sales managers use forecasts to motivate salespeople	Standards or goals are usually the forecast unless obstacles require interim steps to achieve service goals	

Now ask yourself if your company forecasts engagement or retention in any way. This is different than establishing goals because forecasts essentially ask, are we going to make our goals? Forecasting future engagement or turnover is rare, so I will enter that it usually does not occur. Of course, enter that you do develop forecasts if so in Table 3.10.

Table 3.10. Continually-Building Engagement and Retention Processes Chart

Comparative Processes	Sales	Service	Engagement and Retention
1. Convert to dollars	Margins: "This product brings a 22% margin, which results in $4,000 for each sale going right to the bottom line"	Correlations: "For each 2% improvement in our service score, our revenues increase by $124,000"	Results reported in percentages and scores with no correlations to dollars; sometimes include comparisons to benchmarks
2. Establish goals	Essential for revenue generation and defined for total company, sales managers, and sales employees; goals are increased year to year and sometimes quarter to quarter	Drive additional business from current customers and referrals; defined for total company, service managers, and service employees	Most times retention goals either are not set at all or are set for the total organization; engagement goals are rarely established, and past scores and benchmarks serve as standards without specific improvement objectives
3. Train and provide tools	Product training, sales training, collateral sales materials, administrative tools and training to use them	Product training, service training, administrative tools and training to use them	Compensation, benefits, management and supervisory training, surveys, employee programs
4. Forecast future performance	Sales executives use forecasts to reallocate resources and sometimes alert CEOs; sales managers use forecasts to motivate salespeople	Standards or goals are usually the forecast unless obstacles require interim steps to achieve service goals	Forecasts rarely occur

I will present ways to forecast retention and engagement in Chapter 7.

In Table 3.1 that contained our interview questions, Questions 5 through 7 were about accountability and more importantly, consequences. I included several questions about accountability because I suspect that when you asked Question 8 about which process step was most important, you might have heard about accountability then as well.

Accountability requires frequent tracking of achievements

against goals. Sales and service units are tracked daily in most organizations, and reports are issued via online dashboards for many eyes to see.

Accountability related to achieving sales goals brings extremes. Major bonuses are paid to executives, sales managers, and sales personnel when goals are exceeded. Some win cars or family vacations. Those who consistently miss goals lose their jobs. Service accountability brings less glamour but similar risk. Few stories are told of sales workers who lose their jobs over one botched sale, but service employees are sometimes terminated for mishandling emotional situations with clients.

Let's enter this fifth and last comparative process step as "We Hold Employees Accountable to Goals" and write in summary comments for sales and service in Table 3.11.

Table 3.11. Continually-Building Engagement and Retention Processes Chart

Comparative Processes	Sales	Service	Engagement and Retention
1. Convert to dollars	Margins: "This product brings a 22% margin, which results in $4,000 for each sale going right to the bottom line"	Correlations: "For each 2% improvement in our service score, our revenues increase by $124,000"	Results reported in percentages and scores with no correlations to dollars; sometimes include comparisons to benchmarks
2. Establish goals	Essential for revenue generation and defined for total company, sales managers, and sales employees; goals are increased year to year and sometimes quarter to quarter	Drive additional business from current customers and referrals; defined for total company, service managers, and service employees	Most times retention goals either are not set at all or are set for the total organization; engagement goals are rarely established, and past scores and benchmarks serve as standards without specific improvement objectives

3. Train and provide tools	Product training, sales training, collateral sales materials, administrative tools and training to use them	Product training, service training, administrative tools and training to use them	Compensation, benefits, management and supervisory training, surveys, employee programs
4. Forecast future performance	Sales executives use forecasts to reallocate resources and sometimes alert CEOs; sales managers use forecasts to motivate salespeople	Standards or goals are usually the forecast unless obstacles require interim steps to achieve service goals	Forecasts rarely occur
5. Hold employees accountable to goals	Reports issued daily in most organizations; consequences vary with extremes from large bonuses to getting fired	Reports issued daily in most organizations; poor customer service can lead to loss of job	

As we fix our eyes on the blank box for accountability for engagement and retention, what will you enter for your company? In decades of helping organizations improve these areas, I can think of no tangible rewards a manager received specifically for excelling in these areas, nor can I think of a time when a manager was removed from his or her job only because of high turnover or high disengagement.

The unwritten code seems to be, if the manager performs well in other areas but runs off employees or scores low on engagement surveys, it is OK—especially if that manager has been around for years and is seen as otherwise favorable by executives.

Perhaps the following questions are worth asking:

- » If managers have high turnover and low engagement but still make their numbers, might it be that their performance goals are too low?
- » How much higher would their production be if trained employees stayed and performed at their best?
- » And how much higher would our profits be if all managers significantly improved their engagement and retention?

Although no HR terminations come to mind that occurred directly either from high turnover or disengagement, I can think of times when HR executives fell out of favor for failing to stem these tides.

So I will write in summary comments in the open box for this final step while you write in the comments that best describe your company's accountability levels for engagement and retention in Table 3.12. Please make note of consequences too.

Table 3.12. Continually-Building Engagement and Retention Processes Chart

Comparative Processes	Sales	Service	Engagement and Retention
1. Convert to dollars	Margins: "This product brings a 22% margin, which results in $4,000 for each sale going right to the bottom line"	Correlations: "For each 2% improvement in our service score, our revenues increase by $124,000"	Results reported in percentages and scores with no correlations to dollars; sometimes include comparisons to benchmarks
2. Establish goals	Essential for revenue generation and defined for total company, sales managers, and sales employees; goals are increased year to year and sometimes quarter to quarter	Drive additional business from current customers and referrals; defined for total company, service managers, and service employees	Most times retention goals either are not set at all or are set for the total organization; engagement goals are rarely established, and past scores and benchmarks serve as standards without specific improvement objectives
3. Train and provide tools	Product training, sales training, collateral sales materials, administrative tools and training to use them	Product training, service training, administrative tools and training to use them	Compensation, benefits, management and supervisory training, surveys, employee programs
4. Forecast future performance	Sales executives use forecasts to reallocate resources and sometimes alert CEOs; sales managers use forecasts to motivate salespeople	Standards or goals are usually the forecast unless obstacles require interim steps to achieve service goals	Forecasts rarely occur
5. Hold employees accountable to goals	Reports issued daily in most organizations; consequences vary with extremes from large bonuses to getting fired	Reports issued daily in most organizations; poor customer service can lead to loss of job	Tracking occurs but few meaningful consequences for managers or for HR

Experience tells me that if your process experts did not name "accountability" as your company's most important process step, they got it wrong. Research also tells us this, as you will see later in this book when I present accountability solutions in Chapter 8.

The Accountability Lump under the Rug

A primary reason why engagement and retention initiatives fall short is because CEOs fail to hold the right people accountable for improvements. Their logic usually goes like this:

» If employees make stay/leave or engage/disengage decisions because of pay, and HR is in charge of pay, then HR must be accountable.

» If employees tell us they disengage because of communications or recognition, HR should be able to initiate a program to solve these things.

» If HR is in charge of engagement and exit surveys, HR should be ultimately accountable for improving engagement and retention results.

In fact, 86 percent of CEOs look to HR to implement employee programs to improve retention.[6] And in the aforementioned *Economist* study, executives said the top metrics they use for holding HR accountable are employee satisfaction and retention.[7]

If you and your executive team take only one message away from this book, let it be that *the major obstacle to improving engagement and retention is that first-line leaders are not held accountable for it*. Somewhere along the way we all climbed aboard the idea that HR can solve these critical metrics with programs and that leaders' influence is inconsequential, as though first-line leaders are invisible in the day-to-day lives of their employees.

Leader power is so essential to gaining fresh thinking to improve engagement and retention that I will continue to provide research reminders throughout the rest of this book. Otherwise it would be too easy to read about leader power once and then fall back into "program solution" thinking. Addressing leader power in your organization underscores the required courage to develop real solutions, the type of courage referenced by Mark Jin in the Introduction. You can look ahead to specific research references regarding (a) the impact of leaders on how long employees stay, (b) the power of retention and engagement goals for leaders, (c) how leaders who develop trust increase engagement and retention with their teams, (d) specific studies on how leaders influence engagement, and (e) the strength of leader relationships versus the far lesser role compensation plays in engagement and retention. In all, **25** convincing studies will be referenced, beginning with the one that follows.

Leader Power Example #1: Google and the *Fortune* 100 Best Companies to Work For

Since 1998, *Fortune* magazine has announced the winners of its prestigious 100 Best Companies to Work For award. Companies apply for consideration and then learn if they have made the list when the magazine's February edition comes out each year. That edition typically includes a capsule summary of the benefits and programs each winning company offers, usually in a fold-out feature, and in-depth articles about the companies that rate the highest.

Google has topped this list six times, with a four-year win streak from 2012 through 2015. The 2012 edition featured an image of two employees playing ping-pong while others behind them played foosball, with this quote that followed: "the famous perks of the Plex: bocce courts, a bowling alley, eyebrow shaping … 25 cafes, all gratis."[8]

The 2013 Google winning image showed us a young woman on an indoor slide that appeared to connect two floors. This time the quote described even better employee programs and benefits including 100,000 hours of subsidized massages along with "three wellness centers and a seven-acre sports complex, which includes a roller hockey rink; courts for basketball, bocce, and shuffle ball; and horseshoe pits."[9]

For 2014 Fortune positioned Google differently by emphasizing Google's donations indicating "Last year a new program sent employees to Ghana and India to work on community projects."[10] Then for 2015 Fortune emphasized Google's "Baby Bonding Bucks" for all new parents to use during the first three months of their child's life.[11]

The message delivered through pictures and words is clear: *great programs + great benefits = great places to work*. Executives who read these articles must say, "We cannot be exactly like Google but we can make a few changes. Where should we start? Massages? Eyebrow shaping? Horseshoe pits?" Until one reads the fine print at the end of each *Fortune* article, which says the following: "Two-thirds of a company's score is based on the results of the Great Place to Work Institute's Trust Index Survey."[12]

Further digging leads us to learn that the way companies apply for the *Fortune* 100 Best Companies designation is via the website of the Great Place to Work Institute. This institute is the survey arm for many "best places to work" awards, and a quote on its site says the Trust Index Survey measures "employee engagement by surveying employee opinions, attitudes and perceptions on the level of trust between colleagues and between management and employees."[13] The site goes on to say that "trust is the defining principle of great workplaces—created through management's credibility, the respect with which employees feel they are treated, and the extent to which employees expect to be treated fairly."[14]

So here's the scoop. The annual *Fortune* issue of the 100 Best Companies award strongly implies that *programs and benefits* lead employees to see their employers as being great places to work, yet these programs and benefits count for only one-third of the score. The remaining two-thirds is based on the amount of *trust* that managers generate with their teams.

Certainly images of employees on slides or playing ping-pong and references to extreme benefits/eyebrow shaping/horseshoe pits make for sexier magazine stories than something as intangible as trust. One must read the fine print to learn what really makes great companies great. The magazine even provides special icons for each of the 100 companies to indicate whether they provide high pay, domestic partner benefits, onsite fitness centers, or have low turnover. But the only mention of trust is in the fine print at the end of the article, yet trust constitutes two-thirds of the award.

Recall, then, the reference to the Great Place to Work Institute's engagement findings in Chapter 1 where we learned the following:[15]

» Committed and engaged employees who trust their management perform 20 percent better than other employees.

» Companies with committed and engaged employees have half the voluntary turnover rates of their competitors.

» The financial performance of the publicly traded companies on the *Fortune* 100 Best Companies list consistently outperform major stock indices by 366 percent.

We now know that these improvements are based not on programs or benefits but on trust, built daily by managers and supervisors by the way they treat their teams. The lesson is that employees stay and work hard based on *how you treat them rather than on what you give them*. Leaders at all levels, cascading down from the CEO, are the driving forces for building trust with your talent and, as we will see in Chapter 8, they must be held accountable for engaging and retaining their teams.

The Business-Driven Engagement
and Retention Flow Chart

In the next five chapters I will provide real solutions to improve engagement and retention, all mirroring the identical, proven processes your company uses to improve sales and service. Below is Figure 3.2, a flow chart that depicts our work in this chapter, a *process* flow chart at the strategic level that marks our direction for success.

Figure 3.2 The Business-Driven Engagement and Retention Flow Chart

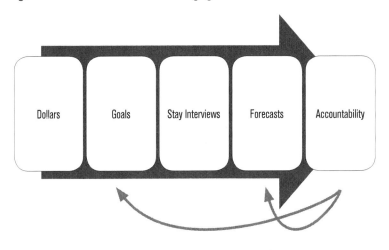

Converting outcomes to dollars, establishing goals, applying stay interviews as our primary solution tool, forecasting success, and holding leaders and others accountable for goals and forecasts now compose our business-driven solution based on the sales and service chassis of organizational success. Specific tactics will follow.

5 Questions/Suggestions for You and Your C-Suite Executives to Overcome HR's Greatest Challenge

1. Tell your C-suite colleagues about your interviews with your sales and service process leaders; then ask them Question #8 in Table 3.1 regarding which process contributes most to goal achievement. If they respond with any answer other than accountability, ask them if they considered accountability when responding.

NOTES: _____

_____

_____

_____

_____

2. Discuss with your top team the degree to which you establish goals for engagement and retention. If your goal-setting is tied to external benchmarks, ask what percentile goal above the median is acceptable.

NOTES: _____

_____

_____

_____

_____

3. Develop a list of managers who have experienced either positive or negative operational consequences that can be traced directly to their engagement and retention performances. Share this list with your top team and ask (a) if they can think of any other managers who should be included and (b) whether additional managers should

have experienced positive or negative consequences based on their engagement or retention performances but so far have not.

NOTES: _____

_____

_____

_____

_____

4. Ask your sales and service process managers to provide known correlative information such as the percentage margin on specific products or the dollar value for improving a specific service metric. Report this information to your top team and ask if they would benefit from knowing similar correlative data for engagement and retention.

NOTES: _____

_____

_____

_____

_____

5. Visit with a sales manager and ask if he or she believes asking salespeople to forecast future sales increases their focus to close those sales. Ask for specific examples and then share this information with your executives. Ask them if they therefore believe managers who forecast their engagement and retention performances will then be more likely to achieve those forecasts.

NOTES: _____

_____

_____

_____

_____

Chapter 4.

Convert Engagement Scores and Turnover Percentages to Dollars

Comparative Processes	Sales	Service	Engagement and Retention
1. Convert to dollars	Margins: "This product brings a 22% margin, which results in $4,000 for each sale going right to the bottom line"	Correlations: "For each 2% improvement in our service score, our revenues increase by $124,000"	Results reported in percentages and scores with no correlations to dollars; sometimes include comparisons to benchmarks

Sort-of-serious warning: This chapter contains mathematics, so science, technology, engineering, or math (STEM) skills are required.

Let's begin this discussion with the end in mind. Starting no later than 90 days from today, you will always report engagement and turnover data in dollars. Survey scores and turnover percentages will also be included, but dollars are the language of CEOs. This will be our first concrete step to move engagement and retention to top-5 metrics and put strong authority behind the solution steps that appear in subsequent chapters.

For those who have ever picked up a cue stick, think of this approach as the two-ball-off-the-six-ball. CEOs will embrace establishing goals and accountabilities for engagement and retention once they fully understand their dollar values.

The villain here is benchmarks. We have become gullible to retention and engagement benchmarks—long heralded as the right comparison metrics—because we believe solutions are scarce—"we just can't pay more"—so any score above the norm becomes an indication of success. If engagement or retention is one hair better than the comparison group, our reaction is we have somehow managed to exceed expectations. But if CEOs saw that sales or service performance is barely above average, they would figuratively pound the management-meeting table until it improved. The differences are (a) they clearly see the pathways to better sales and service but not to engagement and retention, and (b) they know how many dollars are on the table with sales and service but have no dollar values to attach to employees working harder and staying longer.

The Conversation When You Don't Know Costs

Let's present a scenario in which CEOs are presented with turnover data when they do not know costs, when they cannot convert the damage done by turnover into dollars. Below is a real conversation that happens in most companies that if not corrected leads to megadollars being flushed away. We will call it "The Conversation When You Don't Know Costs."

> CEO: Thank you for sharing our monthly turnover data, Rodney. Can you tell me how our turnover compares to our peers'?

> Rodney: We do have that data. As you can see, our annualized turnover is 23 percent, and other companies in our industry have turnover of 25 percent.

> CEO: That's good news, Rodney. We are ahead of our competition, so we must be doing well.

The problem here is that the CEO might have a multimillion dollar turnover problem, but he or she is comforted by knowing the company is ahead of average data representing the competition.

Here is how this conversation unfolds when lost dollars are included in the monthly report:

CEO: Thank you, Rodney, for sharing the turnover data. I see our turnover is running at 23 percent. What is this column that lists dollars that totals to $6.4 million?

Rodney: That's the total annual cost of our employee turnover.

CEO: Our turnover is costing us $6.4 million? We need to make this better!

The difference is that once dollars are involved, CEOs not only understand the importance of the data, but they also become far less interested in comparing their firms' performance to their peers'—as they should.

You can repeat this exchange and substitute employee engagement survey scores for turnover percentages. Like turnover percentages, employee survey scores bring with them no assigned dollar values, so the CEO is again eager to know how scores compare with peers' scores. If the score exceeds the benchmark average, the CEO's false-security response is, "We're doing OK," or worse, "Our engagement score is high." Recalling Gallup's study that at most 31 percent of U.S. employees are engaged, what is the lost value of the remaining 69 percent who are not giving their all in their jobs?[1]

CEOs have a DNA-driven need to see data, and their native language is dollars. Without dollars as a reference, they seek benchmark data that when measuring the impact of turnover and disengagement leads them astray.

One test of whether your executives realize the dollar values of engagement and turnover is to recall if your CFO has ever reported either as a contributing factor to profitability or quality. Think back to your CFO's monthly earnings reports and whether you remember if just one time your CFO said, "Earnings in this division were down last month, and we think that was driven at least in part by its engagement levels, as we saw on the most recent survey results. Employees there are just not performing as they should." A high percentage of us would likely answer no.

Losing 23 percent of your employees can never be acceptable, even in call centers, fast food, or other high-turnover industries. And it can never, absolutely never, be acceptable that 69 percent of your employees do not give their best. Translating these outcomes into dollars makes peer comparisons moot.

Leader Power Examples #2, #3, #4, #5, and #6: Why Do Employees Stay?

The Corporate Leadership Council reported that 22 of the top 25 most effective levers of employees' intentions to stay within an organization were driven by their manager. Examples included accurately assessing employee potential, clearly articulating organizational goals, and encouraging employee development.[2]

Salary.com found that the top two reasons employees stay are managers and co-workers, making clear that *people stay for people.*[3]

Do you think teachers make stay/leave decisions based on pay, lack of career growth, or difficult kids to teach? "When employees stay, it is because of their immediate managers," says the National Education Association. "Teachers will move to or remain in schools with strong administrative leadership."[4]

TalentKeepers studied why employees join versus why they stay. They found employees join for organizational issues such as pay, benefits, or reputation, followed by job-related issues such as schedules, opportunities to learn new skills, or challenging work. But within as little as three months the leading leave or stay reasons shift to supervisors first, followed by job-related issues and then organizational issues.

> Said another way, employees know little about their supervisors when they join, so pay, schedules, and other factors take on greater importance. But shortly after hire supervisors rise to the top of the influence list.[5]
>
> In another study, TalentKeepers found that employees who stay primarily for their supervisors—versus schedules, benefits, or another "thing"—stay longer, perform their jobs better, and are even more satisfied with their pay.[6]

Placing Dollar Costs on Turnover

Let me now present a specific formula for placing dollar costs on turnover. This formula represents years of work, multiple revisions, and ideas gained from other calculators that we found to be helpful but less effective.

The first step is to choose a job for which current turnover most interferes with your organization's success. In other words, choose the job that when employees leave it, profits and productivity are hurt the most.

Then gather a team with representatives from human resources and finance and at least one subject matter expert for the job you are costing. CFOs must involve themselves from the beginning by either participating on this team or by sending a representative who carries their full confidence. Realize from the start that the person who must ultimately approve your cost team's work and sponsor it to the CEO is the CFO, so the CFO ultimately becomes the owner of this process.

CFO sponsorship is essential because CFOs are responsible for critical numbers. They bring authority such that their endorsement of a metric brings locked-in support from the CEO and the executive team. All action steps related to costing turnover should be designed to ultimately gain the full and enthusiastic support from the CFO. Besides, CFOs' jobs are to find coins in the couch. They sleep with notepads on nightstands to jot down 3 a.m. ideas on cutting costs or increasing revenues. Once your CFO learns the real costs of turnover and disengagement, he or she will become your strongest ally to implement the right solutions.

Begin your meeting by discussing this quote attributed to Albert Einstein: "Not everything that counts can be counted, and not everything that can be counted counts."

Based on Einstein's wise words, the key points for agreement are that (1) the team and costing model will be used to develop the closest possible cost for turnover, but there will be limitations, and (2) it is more important that executives agree to the cost than the cost is 100 percent accurate. Said another way, we will develop the best cost of turnover for the appointed job and ultimately all agree on the outcome.

Let's take that last point one step further. The data you develop from your costing process will be used for a long period of time when reporting turnover because all turnover reports from this time forward will include dollar values. These data will be changed only when you have reason to redo the cost analysis. So executives must all concur that the data you develop is right. One crack in the armor six months later in the form of an executive saying "I never really believed in those numbers" will invalidate your work.

Eleven data points are required for the turnover cost model. Seven data points are required to develop the direct costs for exiting the leaving employee and hiring one new employee in this job. Four additional data points are required to measure the lost productivity for both while that job is open and when the new hire is learning the job. In this example we will calculate the cost of losing one nurse. You will see that the cost estimates are extremely conservative.

The first set of these data points, as presented in Table 4.1, provides fundamental job information that will be applied later in the model.

Table 4.1. Data for Calculating the Cost of Turnover

1.	Nurses' annual average compensation and benefits: $75,000 ($312.50 per day based on 240 full-time equivalent—FTE—workdays per year)
2.	Annual average compensation and benefits for all positions: $60,000
3.	Projected nurse exits this year: 200

Next measure the hard dollars costs of exiting one nurse and hiring another:

4.	Separation costs such as exit interviews, administrative costs, separation pay: $100
5.	Vacancy costs such as temporary help and overtime: $2,000
6.	Average acquisition costs for one new hire such as advertising, agencies, employee referrals, travel, interviews, assessments, background checks, reference checks, physicals, bonuses, relocation: $2,900
7.	Placement costs such as new supplies, onboarding days, training days: $3,750 (based on no new supplies and two onboarding days and 10 training days @ $312.50 per day)
8.	Total direct costs: $11,750

Then calculate lost productivity:

9.	Annual revenue divided by the number of FTE employees: $240,000 based on Saratoga Institute data, but replace that figure with your company's actual data
10.	FTE workdays per year: 240 based on Saratoga Institute data, but insert your own number of workdays here if yours is different
11.	Average workdays position open: 20 for our example, but insert your own data here
12.	50% workdays to total effectiveness: 10 for our example, but insert your own data here. This is the number of workdays typical employees need after date of hire to become fundamentally proficient in their jobs to work each day with no one looking over their shoulders, divided by two because they are partially productive each day on an increasing scale

* Published by the Saratoga Institute circa 2006 and serves today as an appropriate conservative estimate.

We apply these data to calculate lost productivity this way:

- We know the daily revenue for each full-time equivalent (FTE) employee in our example is $1,000, as annual revenue per FTE of $240,000 ÷ 240 workdays = $1,000.
- We also know the daily revenue for nurses is $1,250, as nurses earn 25 percent more than average employees, calculated by comparing their $75,000 per year in salary and benefits versus an average of $60,000 per year for all employees.

» From these data we can multiply each nurse's daily revenue value of $1,250 x the number of days the position is open (20), and we then know the lost productivity while the position is open ($25,000).

» Using the same calculation for the lost productivity for the 10 days of ramp-up time while the new nurse is learning the job, there is additional lost productivity of $12,500.

So the total gross lost productivity is **$37,500**.

» Two values must be subtracted from the gross lost productivity to ensure accuracy:

  • The salary and benefits saved during the 20 days the job is open result in a credit of $6,250; this value is determined by multiplying the number of days the job is open (20) x the daily compensation rate ($312.50).

  • And the vacancy cost of $2,000 for temporary help and overtime must also be credited, as these dollars were invested to reduce the amount of lost productivity, and we have accounted for 100 percent of this lost productivity as though no investment was made to improve it.

So the resulting net lost productivity is **$29,250**.

By adding the direct costs and lost productivity, we learn the cost of losing one nurse:

> Direct costs from line #8 in Table 4.1: $11,750
> Lost productivity: $29,250
> **Total cost for losing one nurse: $41,000**

Lost Productivity Costs Must Be Included

Though the direct costs for exiting one employee and hiring another are easier to calculate, the lost productivity costs must be included because this drop-off in productivity due to turnover is usually the greater cost. The model is based on the assumption that all revenue ultimately comes from all employees, so it calculates the lost revenue for the targeted job based on the value of that job to the organization. The job's value is determined by how much the organization chooses to compensate that job relative to other jobs.

Any turnover cost model that omits the lost productivity costs while the job is open and the replacement hire ramps up is overlooking the highest turnover costs. These models result in little more than the cost of hire and fail to represent a fair estimate of the all-in turnover costs.

Our C-Suite Analytics' team has helped hundreds of clients use this model to determine their turnover costs. The great majority of clients and their CFOs have accepted this model in its current form as a legitimate representation of their turnover costs.

The few who did not accept this model suggested that their organizations do not lose productivity while jobs were open because "others fill in." The obvious remedy, then, is to calculate the cost of the extra people whose positions have been established to fulfill the work when positions are open and new hires are ramping up due to turnover. This total annual cost can then be divided by the number of employees in the targeted job who exit in one year, and the resulting value can replace the costs for lost productivity in the model.

The resulting dollar value will be the cost you are paying to shift current staff to cover for openings due to turnover for one exit. You can replace the lost productivity costs from the model with this amount.

Having used nurses as our example, hospitals often have employees they refer to as PRN.[7] This is a group of on-call professionals who are called to fill in during open times due to turnover and vacations and when regular employees are out for other reasons. Hospitals who substitute PRNs for employees who have left or new hires who are ramping up can substitute their costs for each hour of lost productivity, even though overall service levels are likely to be less.

We consider this model a starting point and invite client companies to customize the model by adding other data they might have to make the lost productivity costs more accurate. For example, most organizations know the daily value of salespeople, so they can easily calculate the lost dollars while sales jobs are open and new hires are ramping up, and these dollars should replace the lost productivity dollars that the model would produce.

Total Costs, Total Savings

When we report results from this model, we add at the end the total cost of turnover for the year as well as the dollar values for reducing it. Recalling that if this organization will lose 200 nurses this year, the annual cost of nurse turnover is:

$41,000 x 200 = **$8,200,000**

The savings for reducing nurse turnover by 20 percent = **$1,640,000**

And the savings for reducing nurse turnover by 50 percent = **$4,100,000**

One other way to grab attention is to frame turnover costs for each working day. In this example, our hospital is losing $2,247 each day due to nurse turnover ($8,200,000 ÷ 365 days). Or to make the dollar cost of nurse turnover visible, CFOs can select a similarly priced piece of medical equipment and say, "Imagine if each day we all gathered together and sacrificed this piece of equipment, every day." Or to ask what would be the consequences to an employee who broke this piece of equipment just once by not following procedures.

Now all executives and managers are becoming aware of the full scope of turnover costs as well as improvement opportunities. And whereas the cost of losing one nurse equaling $41,000 might move them to act, more powerful is that they now know the annual cost of turnover exceeds $8 million and that they have a reasonable opportunity to recover greater than $1.5 million in the next 12 months. We typically tell clients we can help them reduce turnover by 20 percent in the first year and by half within three years by using the solutions included in this book.

Over the years we have had a few conversations with CFOs who wish all these dollars could be accounted for in their financial reports. We have the same wish. But just as the precise price of poor service quality will always be elusive, so will the exact cost of employee turnover. This model provides a proxy, a method for measuring the impact of lost productivity that will not appear in financial reports but provides a fair representation. And restricting the cost of turnover to only those dollars that appear in financial statements is greatly underrepresenting its value. This discussion invites reference one more time to Einstein's quote: "Not everything that counts can be counted, and not everything that can be counted counts."

In Chapter 1, I presented data on how many additional patient infections and deaths occur because nursing teams become short-staffed due to turnover. These are good examples of how not everything that counts can be counted.

Why STEM Jobs Cost More to Lose

The model's design underscores the high cost of losing rarely skilled STEM employees in several ways:

»   They are paid more than other employees, and therefore their contribution to revenue is higher.

»   This differential then drives their revenue contribution per day, which becomes the multiplier for the number of days required for hire and the number of ramp-up days.

»   Because STEM jobs often stay open for 90 days and in some cases for up to one year, this high number of open days results in high lost productivity and therefore cost.

» The number of ramp-up days is often high too because the best candidate might not be an initial perfect fit due to the market's shortage of talent.

STEM job candidates might require relocation, hiring bonuses, and headhunter fees if your company continues to use outside recruiters. All these costs aggregate into the high dollars that walk out the door when STEM employees leave. And the model does not accommodate the costs related to product releases being delayed and other project slowdowns that might exceed other lines in the model because "not everything that counts can be counted."

Multiplying Costs for Losing Top Performers

Earlier I gave the scenario of our common reaction to turnover: It depends on who leaves. We know all leavers create costs regardless of their performances because replacements must be recruited, hired, and trained, and the empty chair during hiring and ramp-up represents no productivity versus at least some while the position was filled. Empty chairs also cause others to diffuse their attention from their primary jobs by filling in for others. Even employees you terminate likely did a few duties that are mandatory, that must be done, that now others will have to do in the interim.

But is it fair to say that top performers represent more lost dollars than other employees? One recent broad-based study found that the top 5 percent of workers produced 26 percent of the aggregated firms' total output. The authors concluded, therefore, that top performers produce four times the work of others.[8]

I suggest that these data are meaningful when placing dollar costs on turnover but also that you manage the data with care. Sales organizations know the value of top performers versus others and can easily calculate the cost of losing a top performer. Doing this is far more difficult, though, for jobs that are not so directly tied to revenue. Companies that have identified their top 10 percent or 20 percent of high performers by name might choose to add a multiplier to their potential cost of turnover. Performance ratings, though, are historically far less reliable and should only be used if you believe your company's performance ratings reflect true performance.

Deeper, Mind-Stretching Analyses for Turnover Costs

Some studies stretch our thinking regarding turnover costs as well as the impact turnover has on profitability. Consider if the approaches below can be applied to your organization, especially if you work in the same or a similar industry as these examples.

A study of broker turnover indicated that more than half of brokerage clients changed companies to follow a broker who left.[9] If this is true for your salespeople regardless of your industry, then the cost of salesperson turnover must include the lost revenue from the customers who exit your company due to your losing each salesperson. Salespeople also tend to take other salespeople with them, so the full cost of losing one might equate to the full cost of losing two or three.

If we applied our model to determine the cost of losing one employee in a fast food restaurant, we would probably find the cost to replace and train to be low and the lost productivity costs not much higher. Taco Bell, though, took a different approach. The company studied which variables most drove profitability and found that its top 20 percent stores for retention had double the sales of its bottom quintile and were 55 percent more profitable.[10] This finding implies that customers avoid fast food restaurants because of poor service and that experienced employees provide not just better service than inexperienced employees, but they provide service that attracts customers in contrast to poor service, which drives them away. So another way to gather turnover cost data is to compare the measurable productivity of your same-type departments with low versus high turnover and place a dollar value on the difference.

The third study we will discuss involves outbound telemarketers. This study found that the lost productivity costs of losing one telemarketer were greater than four times the direct turnover costs.[11] So although the direct costs of exiting the leaving employee and hiring and training another are more visible, the indirect costs far exceeded them. We typically find this to be true for any sales position, but what distinguishes this study is that it involved relatively low-paid salespeople who work in call centers rather than higher-paid, commission-based salespeople.

Calculating Turnover's Cost for All Jobs versus One Job

We are calculating costs to report them for infinity. So executives push hard for continuous improvement and managers fully accept that retaining their talent is their responsibility and that they are being held accountable for retention. So, comprehensive reporting requires that complete turnover costs be made known and discussed each month, quarter, and year.

The first step to calculating turnover costs for all jobs is to group all jobs into bands based on their similarities for their turnover costs. Your organization might have 300 jobs or more in your HR information system (HRIS), but it is likely that you can band these jobs together into 10 bands or fewer and then use the model to calculate the turnover cost for each band. The process for banding jobs is to consider their similarities based on the cost items in the model that most affect the total cost of turnover. Here are some considerations:

» Jobs that typically involve relocation might be placed in one band given that this cost is significant.
» Jobs that typically involve external executive search fees might be placed together for the same reason; those that require contingency headhunter fees might also be placed in this band.

» Executive jobs can be grouped because their pay differential compared to other jobs is similarly high.
» Jobs that have similar duties and similar training times might also be combined.
» Nonexempt jobs with similar training times, open position times, and ramp-up times can be grouped.

To go back to our example of a nurse, your hospital might have five different nurse jobs, but they might all be grouped in one band if they have similar acquisition costs, training costs, and numbers of open days to hire and ramp-up days. Similarly, many nonskilled positions can usually be clustered as they have no high costs related to relocation or for search fees and have similar numbers of training days, open position days, and ramp-up days.

Recall that our objective is to determine a reasonable cost of turnover for each job band. Having too many resulting job bands in your turnover report might distract your top-to-bottom management team from focusing on improving retention by debating how many jobs should be in your report and the cost details of each. I recommend making clean decisions you can live with regarding the number of bands and the inclusions of which jobs, so your ongoing focus is to improve retention rather than debate the details of your cost study.

Once you have calculated the cost per exit for each band—with help from HR, finance, and subject matter experts—you can insert these figures into your monthly turnover reports so turnover is reported in dollars for your company and by each department or division, job, length of service, and other factors. You can also develop more extensive annual or even quarterly turnover reports with the emphasis on dollars lost. The example below in Table 4.2 reports the cost of all turnover for one hospital for the previous 12 months.

Table 4.2. Hospital Example: 12 Months Costs, 5 Job Bands

Job Group	Example Jobs	Cost/Exit ($)	Cost/12 Months ($)
Nonskilled	Environmental service, food services, admittance representative	8,503	255,090
Skilled Hourly	Patient care, phlebotomist, secretary	12,627	568,215
Licensed Hourly	Rehab therapy, radio, tech, respiratory therapists	20,388	428,128
Nurses	Inpatient nurses, emergency nurses, surgical nurses	46,250	2,350,000
Exempt	Managers, directors, case managers	57,857	694,284
TOTAL			4,295,717

Source: C-Suite Analytics

Placing Dollar Values on Engagement

In Chapter 1, I presented engagement correlation studies that confirmed the strong link between employee engagement and profitability. Missing, though, was a way to directly apply these studies to your company.

A few years ago Watson Wyatt, a global consulting and research company that is now called Towers Watson, correlated the results of its client companies' performances on an engagement survey against its revenues over a multiyear period.[12] The company then reported, "Analyses show that a significant improvement (one standard deviation) in employee engagement is associated with a 1.9 percent increase in revenue per employee."[13]

Further, Watson Wyatt said, organizations that improved their employee engagement by one standard deviation were associated with a revenue increase of $4,675 for each employee. For a typical S&P 500 organization, this amounts to $93.5 million in additional revenue each year. The breadth of this study provides a statistical basis we can apply to determine the dollar values of engagement for your company. Let's consider as an example the following organization:

» The company earns $100 million in annual revenue.
» It conducted an engagement survey that reported scores on a scale of 1 to 10.
» The company's targeted score was 8.
» Its actual organization score was 7.
» The distribution of scores indicated a standard deviation of 1.

We can then chart the company's outcome in the following way and apply the formula to determine its engagement survey impact in dollars as shown in Figure 4.1.

Figure 4.1. Engagement Calculator: Example

As the graphic indicates, this organization lost 1.9 percent of its annual revenue because its overall survey score was one standard deviation below its targeted score, losing a total of $1.9 million. These are dollars completely left on the table, dollars that CEOs and most CFOs would never consider when reviewing employee survey results without knowing the research behind the cost of engagement or seeing this graph.

Let's now use this same formula but adapt it to one department within this organization; our example will be the technology department as shown in Figure 4.2. Here's the scenario:

» This is the same organization, and it earns $100 million in annual revenue.

» This organization conducted an engagement survey that reported scores on a scale of 1 to 10.

» The organization's targeted score was 8, which was the targeted score for each department too.

» The actual technology department score was 9.

» Distribution of scores indicated a standard deviation of 1.

» The technology department's salaries and benefits are equal to 10 percent of the organization's total salaries and benefits.

Figure 4.2. Engagement Calculator Example, Technology Department

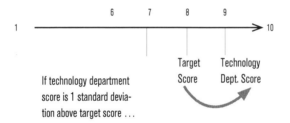

If technology department score is 1 standard deviation above target score …

Target Score

Technology Dept. Score

Technology department is achieving 1.9% of additional revenue (0.019 x $100 million = $1.9 million; $1.9 million x 0.10 = $190,000). Technology department salaries and benefits comprise 10% of organization's total salaries and benefits.

This graphic tells quite a different story. Because the technology department's score was one standard deviation above the targeted score, its dollar value is positive rather than negative. The formula to determine this value begins the same way as we calculated for the entire organization by determining the dollar value for the total company if it had achieved this score of 9, and in this example that value is a positive $1.9 million. Next we multiply this positive value, $1.9 million, by the percentage of company compensation and benefits paid to the technology department, which is 10. The mathematical equation is:

(Company engagement value) x (technology department
compensation and benefits as a percentage of total company
compensation and benefits) = dollar value
$1.9 million x 0.10 = $190,000

The result is that the technology department is bringing in
$190,000 of revenue entirely because the employees there are
more engaged in their work than the level for which the company
set its target. This $190,000 in added revenue is in addition to the
expected performance of the technology department, even though
typical technology departments do not produce revenue. In this case
the added engagement of the technology department team has an
added revenue dollar value of $190,000.

Why did we use each department's total compensation and
benefits rather than their number of employees to determine the
departments' engagement values? Because some departments have
a greater impact on revenue than others, and the model assumes
that top management designs compensation to reward those
employees and those departments that affect revenues the most.
For example, an administrative department could achieve the same
survey score as the sales department and might also have the same
number of employees, but a logical assumption would be that
the sales team would have a greater impact on revenue than the
administrative team. The model accommodates this assumption.

Our examples are designed to use simple computations to
make understanding clear. Most standard deviations will likely be
in fractions and not in whole numbers, but they will work just as
effectively in this model.

Drilling Down to Each Department's and Manager's Engagement Dollar Value Is the Game-Changer

Placing a dollar value on your company's total engagement score
shines light on engagement's total value and will drive your CEO

to expect greater improvements. But placing dollar values on each department's score *and therefore on each department manager's score* helps us claw our way toward individual accountability. Consider right now the consequences for managers whose engagement scores have been below your company's average. What words were said, what actions were taken by that manager's manager or the CEO regarding this score? Might more accountability have been generated if beside that score you were able to add a substantial negative dollar value?

Reporting each leader's positive or negative dollar contribution based on each teams' engagement levels is a wake-up call each CEO needs to hear.

Does This Engagement Cost Calculator Really Work?

Well-respected thought leaders attest to the validity and value of our engagement model, including Gary Borich, Ph.D., Endowed Fellow, Quantitative Methods Program at the University of Texas at Austin:

> The C-Suite Analytics Engagement Calculator[14] is a welcomed, one-of-a kind tool to help organizations fully grasp the value of engaged employees as well as the huge number of dollars left on the table when employees don't give their best. Perhaps its greatest value is that it distinguishes managers who influence engagement from those who do not, in specific dollar values.
>
> This calculator is based on broad-based research and its algorithms have a solid statistical foundation. It can work with any engagement survey and assumes that survey measures engagement in a valid way.[15]

Conducting Correlative Studies to
Measure Engagement's Value

In addition to measuring the dollar values of engagement based on survey scores as described above, values can also be measured by correlating survey scores to important company metrics as shown in Chapter 1. These metrics can include profits, revenues, shareholder returns, stock price, quality, absences, safety, and more. Correlations can also be measured between individual survey items and these metrics.

Data resulting from these studies motivate your CEO to push even harder for engagement improvements. And they remove any arguments that engagement might drive key metrics elsewhere but not here. Now your CFO will begin to regularly report the impact of engagement on these metrics, and subsequently all leaders at all levels will clearly understand that engagement is a first-tier metric.

Who Is Qualified to Conduct These Calculations?

Many large organizations have industrial/organizational psychologists who have been trained in statistics and can conduct all calculations in this chapter. All have studied these quantitative methods and should ultimately be able to follow these formulas.

Smaller organizations can find similarly skilled people either as independent consultants or graduate students in local universities. Professors sometimes moonlight to do this type of work. A detailed online search and a couple of phone calls should lead to several qualified candidates who will perform these calculations on an hourly or project basis.

The dollar investment for these calculations pales relative to moving your executives and managers at every level to see engagement and retention as first-tier profit drivers.

Let's close this chapter by updating our engagement and retention processes relative to the CEO language, which is dollars as shown in Table 4.3. Then move on to our next solution that mirrors how our organizations manage sales and service.

Table 4.3.

Comparative Processes	Sales	Service	Engagement and Retention
1. Convert to dollars	Margins: "This product brings a 22% margin, which results in $4,000 for each sale going right to the bottom line"	Correlations: "For each 2% improvement in our service score, our revenues increase by $124,000"	Results reported in dollars or correlations to propel engagement and retention to top-5 metrics

5 Questions/Suggestions for You and Your C-Suite Executives to Overcome HR's Greatest Challenge

1. In PwC's *Annual Global CEO Survey*, a full 47 percent of CEOs reported they want more information regarding employee turnover.[16] Similarly, executives in the aforementioned *Economist* study said "unavailability of data" was their greatest obstacle to measuring the value of their HR functions.[17] Tell your C-suite executives about these studies and ask what specific data they would like to know. Then also ask if your reporting turnover and engagement in dollars would be helpful.

NOTES: _____
_____
_____
_____
_____

2. Privately share the turnover and engagement calculators with your CFO and ask for his or her input on their effectiveness. Then ask if he or she will support your applying these calculators if you include his or her suggestions. Ask also if the CFO will work directly with

you to conduct calculations or provide someone from the CFO's team whose opinion he or she trusts.

NOTES: _____

_____

_____

_____

_____

3. Ask your C-suite team how much money your company spends on fill-in work others must do while jobs are open due to turnover or for new-hire ramp-up time. Bring an example for a high-turnover job and add any data you have gleaned from using the turnover cost calculator or other sources. Doing so will open their minds to the turnover cost data you and your CFO will report to them later.

NOTES: _____

_____

_____

_____

_____

4. Conduct at least one engagement correlation study by finding the relationship between a critical company metric and your company's score on your engagement survey or on at least one survey item.

NOTES: _____

_____

_____

_____

_____

5. Ask your top sales executive which top performers he or she is especially concerned about losing. Then ask how many other top salespeople they could potentially take with them to their new employers.

NOTES: _____

_____

_____

_____

_____

Chapter 5.

Establish Engagement and Retention Goals for Leaders

Comparative Processes	Sales	Service	Engagement and Retention
2. Establish goals	Essential for revenue generation and defined for total company, sales managers, and sales employees; goals are increased year to year and sometimes quarter to quarter	Drive additional business from current customers and referrals; defined for total company, service managers, and service employees	Most times retention goals either are not set at all or are set for the total organization; engagement goals are rarely established, and past scores and benchmarks serve as standards without specific improvement objectives

Our process chart says retention goals are uncommon and engagement goals are rare. If our CEOs say these metrics really matter, what does it tell us that they do not set goals for them? Probably that being one notch above average, presented as a benchmark, is OK.

Let us imagine that a research team just announced that the top way to improve employee engagement and retention is to reduce employee-contributed health care costs by 5 percent, or to have monthly newsletters instead of quarterly ones, or that vision care was the hot benefit and studies proved time and time again that employees who leveraged their vision care benefit were more likely to give their all to their work.

We wish employee engagement and retention were this simple. But it is not complex, either, when we copy our sales or service processes. Salespeople take products to market and build successful careers by selling them. These products have been honed by product development specialists whereas marketing provides air support with advertising and ground support with collateral. Some salespeople sell better than others, and those who succeed win trips to Hawaii while others might lose their jobs. Few products sell themselves; even BMW salespeople must out-skill their counterparts at Mercedes.

Managers, then, must take their organizations' "employee products" and deliver them in ways that increase engagement and retention. These products include pay, benefits, training, communication, recognition, and all others that companies invest tons of money in each year. Those who manage well not only have strong engagement and retention, but as we saw in Chapter 1, they have greater productivity, too.

The point here is that managers drive their employees' levels of engagement and retention as I have detailed with Leader Power Examples throughout this book. More specifically, it is first-line managers, the supervisors your employees report to directly, who most influence how hard your employees work and how long they stay. Employees' greatest motivation does not come from managers above their supervisors, CEO videos, onboarding presentations, or human resources. It comes from their bosses.

Asking human resources to solve engagement and retention, or worse, holding HR staff solely accountable for engagement and retention, drives entirely wrong solutions in the form of HR-driven programs. Consider the two solution options presented in Figure 5.1 for engagement and retention. Which method does your company choose?

Figure 5.1 Are Your Retention Efforts Driven By Accountabilities or Programs?

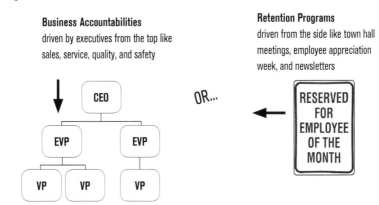

Human resources' influence over employee engagement and retention is strong in the early employment stage, but HR has far less influence after. Consider in your own company how HR drives the recruiting and hiring processes and how in many cases a single HR employee has the most influence on who joins the company. HR's guidance continues by facilitating onboarding and initial training. But then the newly hired employee leaves the HR umbrella—and in most cases leaves structured new-hire processes—and goes to work for his or her supervisor.

Once new employees cross the "fully in their jobs" boundary, HR influences them just as the product development department influences sales. In small companies the HR manager might continue to have relationships with all employees and serve as an informal counselor in ways that affect engagement and retention, but large-company HR professionals are mostly technicians who develop or maintain tools for managers to apply to their teams.

A CEO Short Story about Assigning Responsibility

Consider this story as a way to illustrate how many CEOs see HR's role in engagement and retention.

Two CEOs from different industries meet monthly for lunch to share how they approach various aspects of their businesses. On this day the CEOs discuss employee engagement and retention.

The first CEO begins by saying he has complete faith in his human resources team because it implements the very best compensation and benefits plans, provides ideal training and onboarding, and has designed hiring tools that nearly guarantee that everyone hired is qualified to do their jobs. This HR team also leads the way to provide employee communications, recognition, and career coaching via town hall meetings, newsletters, brown-bag lunches, and employee appreciation week.

The second CEO listens carefully, and then she says, "Our HR people are pretty good, but I rely on our managers to hire, engage, and retain their teams. We realize in our company that managing people is just like managing customers and managing sales, that everything flows from our managers and they are ultimately accountable."

In their next monthly luncheon, the CEOs discuss sales. As usual the first CEO speaks first and describes his tight, top-down sales environment whereby salespeople are trained, coached, and held accountable by their managers. Those who succeed gain rich rewards, and those who fail are coached once and then fired.

Again the second CEO listens carefully and then asks, "If you rely on a staff function such as human resources to engage and retain your employees, wouldn't it make sense, then, to charge your product development team to be accountable for sales?"

Flummoxed by his colleagues' question, the first CEO says, "It sounds crazy to hold employees who work in a back room here in headquarters accountable for customer outcomes when we have salespeople who are in direct presence of customers and have the deepest relationships with them."

To which the second CEO agrees, saying "I just thought that if you believe human resources has more impact on employees' levels of engagement and retention than their managers, you might also think your employees in product development have more impact on sales than your salespeople."

These approaches are starkly different. We encounter this discussion every day when working with clients and, although the discussions take slightly different forms, they boil down to this fundamental conundrum: Why is it that organizational results for employee engagement and retention are often left in the hands of human resources when all other critical business metrics are assigned to those managers and employees who most influence business outcomes, excluding employee engagement and retention?

Leader Power Examples #7, #8, #9, #10, and #11: The Power of Retention Goals

Which of the following cut hospital nurse turnover by 41 percent:

» Providing stellar new programs such as onsite child care and flexible scheduling?

» Asking nurse managers to achieve nurse retention goals?

In its report titled *Hardwiring Right Retention,* the Health Care Advisory Board of the Advisory Board Company told of one hospital that reduced turnover by 41 percent by setting retention goals for managers and holding them accountable. Peer hospitals took a different route by implementing seemingly attractive employee programs but found absolutely no improvement.[1]

The report describes programs such as performance pay, better communications, onsite child care, and flexible scheduling as "nice, but not about turnover" and recommends that hospitals "hold nurse managers accountable to retention goals."

Monster.com studied retention solutions and made its first recommendation: "Make supervisors more accountable for worker retention by tying their compensation to retention performance." It also reported only 11 percent of HR managers indicate their supervisors are held to retention goals in their organizations.[2]

A study by the National Commission on Teaching and America's Future provided clear direction on how to improve teacher retention by recommending "amend NCLB [No Child Left Behind] to hold school leaders accountable for turnover and its costs."[3]

Retention goals would also help solve turnover across the globe.

Kenexa studied workers across six countries and found employees were three times more likely to state an intention to leave if they have a manager who is doing a poor job leading their teams or organizations. Impact is even higher in India and China.[4] Additionally, the Society for Human Resource Management (SHRM) and Development Dimensions International (DDI) studied retention in China and found three of the top four retention drivers are directly related to leadership: having a good manager, being recognized for individual contributions, and having great company leadership. They also found that compensation alone is not sufficient for retaining valued talent.[5]

Why Goals Really Matter

In *Rethinking Retention in Good Times and Bad*, I detailed the processes we put into place to help Hilton's call centers cut turnover by 20 percent each month for the first four months we worked together.[6] This extraordinary improvement resulted from creative, fresh-thinking advances in hiring, onboarding, redesigning of supervisors' roles, and other changes. But looking back, I am convinced the single best solution involved setting a goal.

Hilton's HR team had studied turnover from many angles but not by length of service. We counted early exits from a spreadsheet and found that half the new hires had not reached 90 days of service in any of their centers. Most HR professionals would say fix hiring and onboarding, and we did make improvements there. The more powerful step, though, involved the CEO sending one e-mail to the center directors saying he would begin tracking their performances against a goal that 75 percent of new hires must reach 90 days of service, immediately.

Call centers assign extraordinary attention to metrics, in part because technology gives leaders so much data. It is as though the term "leaderboard" was invented there. So a new goal was introduced literally overnight that sent center managers scrambling to finish at the top of their leaderboards rather than at the bottom on new-hire retention. Though we suggested 90-day retention solutions that they readily accepted, these managers also conducted brainstorming sessions with their direct reports, all for one purpose: to win.

Most people see goals as a way to measure whether initiatives succeed or fail. When setting goals for engagement and retention, *the goals become solutions by themselves.* The Hilton story underscores how ambition to achieve goals brings out previously unseen ideas and high-level problem-solving skills. Goals drive leaders to move from being one notch above average to performing at their best.

Goals bring focus. Most leaders at all levels are skilled enough to fulfill our reasonable requests as long as they know where those requests sit in the priority queue relative to other job demands. No organization can solve engagement and retention without establishing goals and reinforcing to managers at all levels that achieving them is essential for their individual success.

The Engagement and Retention Goal-Setting and Accountability Chart

Goals mean little unless names are attached to them. Saying "we will reduce turnover by 10 percent this year" as a team usually means no one person is accountable. One way to think about goals is that they bring light. But whereas team goals bring *diffused* light, individual goals bring laser-focused attention to achievement. This is a time when saying "you" or "I" is better than saying "we."

Recommendations presented in Table 5.1 are by necessity one-size-fits-all, but of course each organization must find its own way. The discussion-starters here are based on data presented throughout this book and my own experience with developing goals. These approaches seem reasonable, and they will ultimately drive the right behaviors.

Table 5.1. The Engagement and Retention Goal-Setting Chart

Metric	Recommended Goal-Setting Methodology	CEO	Direct Supervisors and All Managers above Them, Including C-suite Executives	Executive-level HR	HR Recruiters	Trainers
Engagement	Continuous annual 20% increase of top-box score	Yes	Yes	Yes	No	No
All Turnover	20% annual decrease until annual turnover is 10% or less	Yes	Yes	Yes	No	No
First-Year Turnover	20% annual decrease until first-year turnover is 10% or less	Yes	Yes	Yes	Yes	Yes
High Performers/High Potentials	Retain 95% percent each year	Yes	Yes	Yes	No	No

Here is the thinking behind each line.

For "Engagement," the goal must address only top-box scores because we learned in Chapter 1 that employees who score in the top box contribute far more productivity than those who score in the middle or low boxes. Recall that many survey companies present your scores as one number that includes both the top and middle boxes, so you must ask them to begin reporting a top-box score, and if they provide benchmarks, to compare your score to other companies' top-box scores. The recommended goal is to continuously increase the percentage of employees who score in the top box by 20 percent each year, regardless of how often you survey. Consider benchmarks as comparison points only if you can learn how your company benchmarks against peer companies for percentage of employees who score in the top box. If these data are available, aim to be in the 90th percentile or higher. But if you cannot learn how your company compares to peers for percentage of employees who score in the top box, I suggest completely ignoring the benchmarks.

Those accountable for achieving your engagement goal should include the CEO, direct supervisor and all managers above that supervisor, and the senior HR leader. This same group is accountable for all four recommended metrics presented here. The reasons for CEO and all manager accountability are obvious; the powerful impact leaders have on engagement and retention is presented throughout this book. Executive-level HR professionals are included because (a) they define all people-management processes, including how employees are hired into their organizations, and (b) they provide skill-building and tools for leaders to select, coach, and hold their teams accountable. I believe HR leaders having accountability also ratchets up their identification of nonperforming managers and their subsequent coaching of their executives to address them.

Executive-level HR professionals, though, should be held no more accountable than the CEO and the other members of the C-suite team. And those C-suite team members should also be accountable for all employees below them on the chart.

But regardless of the power held by the CEO, top managers, and the senior HR leadership team, the greatest accountability must rest on the shoulders of the direct supervisor, as we have learned here that this person has the greatest bearing on engagement and retention outcomes.

For "All Turnover," the recommended goal is to decrease

turnover by 20 percent annually until annual turnover reaches 10 percent or below. The important distinction here is to include *all turnover* in reports, goal-setting, and progress toward goals rather than to set separate goals for and segment out desirable/undesirable or controllable/uncontrollable turnover. The reasons for this recommendation are (a) all turnover is costly and creates turbulence, and (b) real turnover reasons are hard to discern. A third reason for including all turnover is the most pragmatic. When all exits count, supervisors tend to hire much more carefully rather than risk early turnover that will hurt their goal achievement. If terminated employees are not included, supervisors tend to make risky hires and sometimes procrastinate on taking performance actions on those they should not have hired, and your organization ends up retaining poor performers.

"First-Year Turnover" is a broad label for setting retention goals to ensure you increase the percentage of new hires who stay during your "tipping point." Your tipping point is the length of time after hire when early turnover peaks. For example, fast food and call centers might study their own turnover data and learn that employees who stay the first 90 days tend to stay at least two years. Banks, on the other hand, hire recent college graduates into management training programs and find these new hires must learn so much during their first two years that they only see a return on their investment beginning in year three. So banks might extend this category of "First-Year Turnover" to three years for trainees.

The recommended goal is to reduce tipping-point turnover by 20 percent each year until annual turnover reaches 10 percent. HR recruiters are included in this goal entirely because by being included, they will sharpen their eyes to screen out applicants who show early exit signs and also remind supervisors that they must hire candidates who will help them achieve their first-year retention goals. Certainly some early turnover is outside of the HR recruiter's influence because the recruiter cannot control how an employee is treated post-hire, but the trade-off is having that recruiter focused on retention from the start. Large organizations that have multiple recruiters filling identical jobs are in perfect positions to position these recruiters against each other to see who can influence early retention the most.

Trainers are also included in the "First-Year Turnover" goal. This is most effective when designated trainers conduct new-hire training for one week or longer and not only observe how the candidate learns the material but witness fundamental skills such as arriving on time, having zero or few absences, focusing on work, participating in class, and working well with others. Participating in the new-hire goals changes the trainers' reaction to poor performance from "I didn't hire them and don't have to work with them" to "I can't graduate them if I think they won't stay or perform effectively." Being extremely driven by numbers, many call centers often establish a goal for trainers that they must graduate 85 percent of their class participants. Better would be to tell them to graduate 0 percent if none of them will stay.

"High Performers/High Potentials" is the name for the last group. This designation applies only if your organization has identified high-performing employees or high-potential employees by name, and if they represent no more than one quarter of your entire employee population. Performance ratings are usually not a good measure to identify high performers because managers assign these ratings inconsistently. The goal for retaining these employees is recommended to be high because they deliver an extreme amount of your productivity.

The ideal measure for turnover against goals is to annualize year-to-date turnover. This presents the data in a way that says, "If your retention performance stays on this track, your performance will be this number," so it invites the manager to improve. The opposite is to present rolling 12-month data, which instead communicates, "Here is your past performance, and you cannot change it."

Note that except for the reference to top-box engagement

scores, all these goal-setting methods are improving on current performance rather than exceeding benchmarks. Great companies continuously and relentlessly improve against themselves and find little comfort in inching ahead of a competitor.

Goals Must Reflect Your Company's Strategy

While the generic chart in Table 5.1 provides guidelines, specific goals must align with your organization's charted directions. For example, you might establish a higher retention goal for technology workers because they are the backbone of product development. Or recognize that night-shift retention might present a greater challenge and therefore establish less-aggressive goals. One-size-fits-all goals are by far easier to track but might not lead to the best company outcomes.

A Small Part of Engagement and Retention Is Luck

Let us acknowledge the times you know when employees have left your company for reasons other than their supervisors. These leave reasons might be about family member health, spouse relocation, or employees whose real quit reasons are to stay home with children or return to school.

A small percentage of employees are totally focused on pay, and they do not stay anywhere for long. Others slip through your hiring processes and cannot motivate themselves. Another small percentage cannot handle authority in any form. A few others disdain the structure of schedules and deadlines. Some yearn to work on their own and find a path to do so. And there are those who just tire of doing the same thing and cannot find different paths in their current companies.

Some employees will quit or give less than their all even if their supervisors are highly effective with other employees. But the data on supervisors clearly direct us to focus our main solutions through them. This again is similar to how top-level salespeople sometimes lose sales despite their best skills and efforts because prospects sometimes choose another provider. But just as top salespeople continue on and have more success than their peers, your best managers will over time have better retention and engagement than their peers.

That is why retention and engagement goals are never set at 100 percent. Stuff happens—but less negative stuff happens to the best supervisors.

How Frequently Must Engagement Scores Change?

Another unspoken-but-pivotal issue regarding goals and accountability centers on the usual infrequency of engagement surveys. Three of the four metrics listed in Table 5.1 are about turnover, and most organizations provide a turnover report each month. Engagement reports, though, must be tied to engagement survey frequency, and many studies tell us this is usually one year for some companies and two years for others. The obvious question, then, is can you think of any other top-tier metric in your company that stays dormant for at least a full year with no in-between measure?

Employee environments change quickly because of reorganizations, new policies, layoffs, turnover that takes mentors and top performers away, and most importantly changes of leaders. Surveys must therefore be conducted more frequently to bring necessary data and simply to be more meaningful.

Most importantly, how many managers will really hunker down to improve engagement if you tell them their low score is suddenly more significant but they have one year to improve it? Or two years? Or they better improve on the next survey, but we do not know yet when that survey will be? Those managers who seek excuses for low scores the next time can then easily find them in the form of "my responsibilities shifted," "my most positive employees transferred," and others that you have heard before.

The primary obstacle here is that most engagement surveys are too long. They are designed to find micro issues rather than macro ones, but the trade-off is they can only be conducted annually or less frequently, which is too infrequent. The solution, then, is to narrow your survey to a maximum of 15 items and conduct it as frequently as once per quarter. Many companies can insert these questions into employees' computers such that when they turn their computers on, the survey appears, and they can have one or a few days to complete the fewer-than-15 questions.

Objections could be (a) we are asking for too much employee time, or (b) we will build higher-than-we-want expectations. One way to reduce employee time is to survey 25 percent of your employees each quarter. These 25 percent can be distributed in a way that includes 25 percent of each manager's team. This way, each employee is surveyed only once per year, and each manager receives a fresh engagement score every quarter.

And for managers who remain concerned about building expectations, would you have the same concern when conducting customer surveys? Maybe the underlying belief is that customers have reasonable expectations but employees do not—that employees do not understand the realities of our business and therefore want much better pay, benefits, and other unattainable things. My experience is that few employees think this way, and most want duties they like, colleagues who pull their fair share, and managers they trust.

Communicating Goals with Care

Much of this book so far has been about presenting evidence that leaders must be responsible for their talent. Use information presented here, then, to help managers cross that bridge to gain a far deeper understanding of why their having engagement and retention goals makes sense. These details should be delivered by the CEO or another high-level operations executive. Here is the presentation sequence I use with our clients:

1. Costs. Conduct cost studies as detailed in Chapter 4, so you can display turnover costs by job or for your entire company for each year, month, and day; supplement these data with engagement dollar studies you conduct internally or, if you have not done these yet, supplement with several engagement studies presented in Chapter 1.

2. Leader power. Present several of the leader power studies that are contained in most chapters, but more importantly tell stories of leaders who have succeeded or failed in your company because they kept/engaged or lost/disengaged their talent; names of course should only be included for those who have performed well.

3. Share the top-down goals. Managers must know that they are part of an overall top-down management initiative rather than feel singled out as "the cause of the problem." Tell managers the CEO's accountabilities to the board, the top team's accountabilities, and the accountabilities for those managers who are immediately above this group; it is essential they leave the room believing "we are all in this together" and "if those above me are willing to accept these goals, then it must be OK."

4. Tell HR's goals too. This is the right time to draw clear lines as to what HR is accountable for and what outcomes managers must own; report HR's goals, but also use the product development analogy to make clear that HR develops tools for leaders and then leaders must own their talent, especially after hire.

5. Display report samples, frequencies, and consequences. I will address these in Chapter 8.

Let's close this chapter by updating our engagement and retention processes relative to establishing goals for engagement and retention in Table 5.2, and then move on to our next solution that mirrors how our organizations manage sales and service.

Table 5.2.

Comparative Processes	Sales	Service	Engagement and Retention
2. Establish goals	Essential for revenue generation and defined for total company, sales managers, and sales employees; goals are increased year to year and sometimes quarter to quarter	Drive additional business from current customers and referrals; defined for total company, service managers, and service employees	Engagement and retention goals are established for leaders at all levels, including HR

5 Questions/Suggestions for You and Your C-Suite Executives to Overcome HR's Greatest Challenge

1. Ask your CEO how much he or she believes *individual* engagement and retention goals and accountabilities will drive improved manager behavior versus goals only at the organizational level. Then with permission share this discussion with others on your C-suite team.

NOTES: _____

_____

_____

_____

2. Tell your C-suite executives stories you heard from sales and service process leaders regarding how goals inspired individual employees to succeed. Ask them if these same types of goals would drive better manager performance to improve engagement and retention.

NOTES: _____

_____

_____

_____

_____

3. How can you adapt the recommended goals presented in this chapter to your company to make them more meaningful for your C-suite executives?

NOTES: _____

_____

_____

_____

_____

4. What data and other evidence can you present to your CEO to convince him or her that he or she should be accountable for engagement and retention?

NOTES: _____

_____

_____

_____

_____

5. Review your hiring processes in detail. If you are going to ask your recruiters and trainers to accept first-year retention goals, how can you improve these processes to hire applicants who stay?

NOTES: _____

_____

_____

_____

Chapter 6.

The Power of Stay Interviews

Comparative Processes	Sales	Service	Engagement and Retention
3. Train and provide tools	Product training, sales training, collateral sales materials, administrative tools, and training to use them	Product training, service training, administrative tools, and training to use them	Compensation, benefits, management and supervisory training, surveys, and employee programs

Cure-All. Antidote. Touchdown. Eureka.

I was a latecomer to the stay interview bandwagon. I had heard about stay interviews, read a few articles about them, and ultimately included a few pages about their benefits in *Rethinking Retention in Good Times and Bad*.[1] I have learned since that they are the keystone, the linchpin, the superglue that connects traditional fixes like exit and engagement surveys to the processes we use for sales and service.

7th Inning Advice

Christopher Anzalone is responsible for book publishing for SHRM, the Society for Human Resource Management. A few years ago SHRM's annual conference was held in San Diego, and one evening Chris and I scored great tickets to a San Diego Padres game. During the seventh inning Chris gave me career-changing advice that I resisted at first. That evening began Chris's odyssey to convince me to write a stay interview book. Chris's punchline went like this:

> HR executives are learning that engagement surveys just lead to more employee programs, but employees don't stay and don't engage because of programs. Think of it this way. When employees say they want more recognition, why would we think they want to watch someone else win employee of the month or go to an employee appreciation picnic? What they really want is for their supervisor to tell them when they do something well. If you write this book you will start a trend.

Chris's logic cut right through the summer night, yet the overall concept seemed too simple. Will managers really meet with employees, ask the right questions, and act on what they hear? Isn't basic Q&A something left over from the '70s? The story's outcome is that I relented and wrote *The Power of Stay Interviews for Engagement and Retention*,[2] which has become the top-selling SHRM-published book.

The Magic: Stay Interviews as a Process

Let's start with a definition: A stay interview is a structured discussion a leader conducts with each individual employee to learn the specific actions he or she must take to strengthen that employee's engagement and retention with the organization.

Stay interviews are winning tactics because they:
- » Bring information that can be used today.
- » Focus on individual employees, including top performers.
- » Put managers in the solution seat instead of HR, .

Stay interviews must be implemented *as a process* rather than as regular soft-skills training. Many companies offer soft-skills training courses in situation management, communication skills, and career coaching but do not back them with processes to ensure leaders put these well-intended skills into practice. The result is that leaders score classes with high marks and then leave class with the option to change their behaviors—or not.

Stay interviews as a process must include at least the following requirements:

» Asking the right five questions that address key issues related to engagement and retention.

» Schedules to ensure managers conduct stay interviews at least once per year with continuing employees and twice with new hires.

» Cascading to ensure top executives go first and engage their direct reports by modeling the ideal stay interview experience.

» Scheduling so stay interviews happen separately from performance discussions.

» Stay plans that each manager completes that include manager and employee commitments and timelines.

» Identified stay and potential leave reasons that can be aggregated to summarize data for departments and organizations.

» Forecasts, which I will describe in Chapter 8.

» Training for leaders at all levels to conduct stay interviews by learning to listen, take notes, probe, take responsibility, and develop glue-making, engagement-developing stay plans.

Defining stay interviews as a process requires saying what they are *not*. They are not HR conducting focus groups with new employees after 90 days. They are not "rounding" meetings where managers stop by for five minutes with a few scripted questions. They are not development-planning meetings that assume having a career is the most important goal for all employees. They *are* structured meetings focused on the employee: "What will it take for you to stay here longer and become more engaged?"

Scary, some would say. Do we really want to know these answers, especially when looking an employee in the eye? Isn't this why we conduct anonymous surveys, so we can report back on the survey items we choose versus on all of them? Or provide generalized responses by e-mail, so we can skim over those awkward subjects like pay, promotions, and schedules?

Leader Power Examples #12, #13, #14, and #15: Trust-Building Skills Are No. 1

As employees we instinctively know that trusting our managers leads to good things. But a quick literature review reinforces that building trust is by far the absolutely fundamental skill leaders must build to engage and retain their teams.

Leadership IQ found that a full 32 percent of employees' decisions to stay were based on how much these employees trusted their supervisors.[3]

Walker Information found that employees' loyalty was most influenced by employees' perceptions of fairness, care and concern, and trust at work.[4]

Sirota surveyed over 64,000 employees to learn their expectations when they join companies. The answers—be treated with respect, be dealt with equitably, and gain a sense of connection on both work and personal levels—applied equally to young and older workers.[5]

We learned in Chapter 3 that Google has won top slot in the *Fortune* 100 Best Companies to Work For more than any other company, a total of six times out of 18 years for the award. We learned, too, that the main pathway to win is to have leaders at all levels who build trust with their employees. And connecting the dots to Chapter 1, we learned that public companies that have finished in the *Fortune* 100 Best consistently outperform major stock indices by 366 percent.

All of these data prompt the question: What do Google's leaders do that makes them so effective in their jobs? Fortunately, Google conducted an in-house, data-driven study on what makes their leaders

at all levels most effective and rank-ordered eight leadership qualities in
importance, top to bottom:

> Technical expertise—the ability, say, to write computer code
> in your sleep—ranked dead last among Google's big eight.
> What employees valued most were even-keeled bosses
> who made time for one-on-one meetings, who helped
> people puzzle through problems by asking questions, not
> dictating answers, and who took an interest in employees'
> lives and careers.[6]

Let's spotlight those three most important traits:[7]
- » "Even-keeled bosses who made time for one-on-one meetings."
- » "Who helped people puzzle through problems by asking questions, not dictating answers."
- » "And who took an interest in employees' lives and careers."

One can make the case that these three behavioral traits describe
great people-managers who drive great profits. These three traits aptly
describe stay interviews too.

The Five Highly-Researched, Right Questions to Ask

We train managers to ask just five questions and then probe, probe,
probe to uncover each employee's detailed answers. These questions
have been researched and road-tested many times and they are:

1. *When you come to work each day, what things do you look
forward to when you commute to work each day?* This starts the
discussion positively and focuses the employee on daily activities.

2. *What are you learning here?* This says your learning is
important to me if indeed it is important to you. Some employees
want detailed career plans and others just want to do their jobs well
and go home.

3. *Why do you stay here?* Few employees can answer this question without pondering and probes but unlocking this answer provides the holy grail for future emphasis

4. *When was the last time you thought about leaving our team? What prompted it?* This discloses hot buttons and degree of urgency for solutions

5. *What can I do to make your experience at work better for you?* This final question sweeps up loose ends that might have been missed … and probing again is essential for success.

We recently surveyed managers who have conducted many stay interviews to learn among other things, what types of improvements do employees want the most? For those who think employees will want more pay, benefits, or other things that make us squeamish there is good news: The most popular topic was improved work processes. Employees want their managers' help to perform their jobs better and go home feeling more accomplished. Maybe stay interviews should be called productivity interviews.

Overcoming Stay Interview Objections

Since writing the stay interview book, our company has trained thousands of leaders to conduct stay interviews as a process, resulting in turnover falling by up to 70 percent in the first year. Gaining this work has required listening to a few chief HR officers' (CHROs') objections about why stay interviews will not be accepted in their companies. The CHROs usually sound as if they are role-playing for their C-suite executives, anticipating the objections they are certain will come their way.

Borrowing another comparison to sales processes, salespeople learn early how to overcome customer objections to close the sale. Recalling Mark Jin's line in the Introduction, this is one of the "courage" parts. Here are the top five objections you will face.

Objection No. 1: Our Managers Are Way Too Busy To Meet With Employees One-On-One. They Don't Have Time.

Response: Yeah, they sure are busy. And when you consider the huge dollars on the table for engagement and retention and the powerful roles our mangers play to engage and retain their teams, I suggest we look at what they do with their time. We should examine all those standard meetings, ineffective processes, and other things that tie up their time and decide which ones to end. And the time they spend interviewing candidates for open jobs due to high turnover.

It makes sense that some managers will see conducting stay interviews as "another thing to do." Maybe we should show them how much disengagement and turnover cost our company and the research regarding the strong roles they as managers play to improve engagement and turnover. We could ask them what activities they currently do that are less important than conducting one stay interview per year with each employee and two stay interviews with new hires. I think they would tell us how to solve this objection.

We make special efforts to protect salespeople and sales managers from attending less-crucial meetings so they can focus on sales. Maybe we should take the same approach with all managers and reduce their time spent on less effective processes so they can actually coach their teams.

Objection No. 2: We Don't Want to Hear About Things We Can't Fix. Everyone Will Want a Raise.

Response: I agree with the "things we can't fix" part. I have wondered in fact if we should abandon our engagement survey for the same reason. That is one good thing about exit surveys: We can learn what employees wanted, but we no longer have to give it to them.

Let's think about the different ways we treat our employees versus how we treat our customers. I know marketing always wants to know what customers think, and so do our salespeople who are compensated for customer renewals. They have learned how to provide extra services for those who deserve them.

I think it is the same with employees. Most employees I know have reasonable expectations, and they understand we are in business to make a profit. A few will ask tough questions about pay and staffing levels, but we can prepare our managers to handle those questions. Employees who want more money will be told what they have to achieve to earn it. Those who think we need more staff are usually saying they work too many hours, and our managers have to become closer to their work to help them manage it better. And those who want to learn new things or be considered for different jobs need to tell us so we can help them do so.

If we expect managers to own their talent, they must step up and address these issues. And we can coach them to do so. They will be up to the task. And besides, when would you rather hear these concerns, during stay interviews when we can address them or during exit interviews when employees are walking out the door?

Objection No. 3: If We're Going to Do Stay Interviews, Shouldn't HR Do Them Instead of Managers?

Response: No. I have shared with you the power that first-line leaders have over employees' decisions to stay or leave and engage or disengage. HR cannot be the bridge, the arbitrator, that steps into the abyss and translates what employees want from their leaders, or worse, become accountable for new programs to address what employees say. In great companies leaders own their talent. We have designed engagement and retention goals and their resulting accountabilities for leaders. Now is not the time to go backward and ask HR to become surrogate leaders. Let HR do what HR does and leaders do what leaders do—lead their teams.

Objection No. 4: Do You Really Think Employees Are Going to Look Their Supervisors in the Eye and Tell Them What They Want? What if Employees Don't Trust Them?

Response: If our leaders cannot build trust, they should not be leaders. Those who are trained to conduct stay interviews effectively and who ask, listen, take notes, accept responsibility, and develop good stay plans will build trust. HR and their managers will be there to coach them. But leaders who short-cut the process or who lack fundamental management skills like listening and problem-solving will tell us by their outcomes they are in the wrong job. Their problems will not be about an inability to conduct stay interviews but instead about their filling a chair that we should not permit them to fill.

Objection No. 5: This Just Doesn't Seem Like a Fit with Our Culture.

Response: Please tell me more about that. Is the "fit" problem that leaders should not own their talent? Or that HR should substitute for leaders while leaders are doing whatever it is they do besides engaging and retaining their teams? Or might it be that our culture comes up short on accountability, which is another way of saying we do not have the courage to hold leaders accountable so we can build a great company?

Respected research tells us that year after year companies fail to increase engagement among their employees and that they keep spending more and more money to do so. I think this is a clear sign that the basic direction is way off track, and that relying on HR programs to fix engagement has failed. Talent is becoming far more scarce, so retention is critical too. Those executives who refuse to hold leaders accountable and require them to put the right tools into practice risk performing in the middle of the pack or worse. None of us want to work for or lead one of those companies.

A Candid Moment

A few senior HR professionals tend to say that stay interviews will not work in their companies because managers do not have the time or that stay interviews are not part of their culture. This is code for either "I'm afraid to ask my CEO" or "My CEO doesn't hold managers accountable." Many HR leaders who have implemented stay interviews have convinced their executives by leveraging the data in previous chapters regarding two different types of impact: (a) engagement and retention on profits and (b) effective supervisors on how engaged their teams become and how long they stay.

What Is the Single Most Important Leader Skill for Engagement and Retention? Building Trust!

The management shelves in our few remaining bookstores hold titles about recognition, communication, feedback, and career coaching, but all these activities bring emptiness if employees do not trust you. Let me prove this in two ways.

My late colleague Fred Frank designed and administered an instrument to measure the importance of trust that led to indisputable conclusions. Fred asked employees from scores of companies to rank-order 10 individual and positive leadership skills, asking which skills would most influence you to stay with a hypothetical leader—in other words, which skills mean the most to you regarding retention. The skill list included positive recognition, feedback, communication, career coaching, building trust, and five others. The result was that when aggregating the data for each company, building trust finished at the top every time. If building trust finished first 70 percent of the time, we would say it was dominant, that building trust is for certain the top skill required for retaining employees. But building trust finished first every time.[8]

Now I ask you to apply this idea to your own career with a different exercise. Think about the best boss you ever had and then the worst boss you ever had. Imagine them split-screen like when watching CNN and consider the feelings you had when working for each. I would bet that you trusted your best boss and did not trust your worst boss. And also that your best boss had shortcomings you easily overlooked, and your worst boss had strengths you were blind-folded to, that you could not possibly see.

I would also bet that you were most engaged and most likely to stay when working with your best boss. Best bosses tend to listen attentively, sincerely consider your input, and apologize when they are wrong. They also support the company's policies rather than consistently throw upper managers under the bus, even if it requires acknowledging they might not understand an executive's decision, but they also know those above them know things others do not.

When working with groups, I ask participants to do this best boss/worst boss exercise, and some describe a time when a boss broke trust with them. I then ask (a) how did that make you feel? and (b) how did that make you change? Many say they worked less hard, devoted fewer hours to work, and ultimately left.

Leaders at all levels who build trust will see stay interviews as another tool in their toolkit to engage and retain their teams. Others might initially object, failing to see the value. Many of those initial objectors will later leverage stay interviews to build trust with their teams, but a few of them will make clear by their outcomes that they cannot and therefore should not be in leadership positions.

What Do Stay Plans Look Like?

Here are three common stay interview outcomes and real-world action plans that result:

Topic No. 1: I'm bored and want to learn something new in my job. Purchasing looks interesting to me.

Stay plan: Joan in purchasing has agreed to coach you one hour per week for six weeks to teach you the fundamentals of purchasing. Then you and I will meet, so I can understand what you've learned and how to help you apply it to your career.

Background: The manager probed to understand what the employee wanted to learn and asked for one week to develop a plan. The manager considered alternatives to helping the employee learn purchasing and ultimately collaborated with the purchasing supervisor, Joan, to form a solution. Too often "development" becomes linked to career ladders, external courses, and detailed career plans. But oftentimes development does not require an external course or expense, as most companies are rich with a variety of talented people. We just need to ask for help.

Topic No. 2: I can't get out of the office in time to pick up my child in day care without incurring a late fee.

Stay plan: The manager reshuffled work among the team to ensure the employee left on time each day.

Background: At first this solution seems too simple, but many times employees face problems that are so big to them that they choose not to share them, and instead sometimes they seek jobs in other companies as solutions. And oftentimes workloads become uneven in part because we tend to give more to employees who produce more work.

Topic No. 3: I need a promotion to management, or I fear I must leave to get one somewhere else.

Stay plan: The manager proposes a six-month development plan to the employee.

Background: Consider a top programmer with solid communications skills whom some executives would rather retain as a programmer but who comes forward to say he or she can do more. Learning this is a critical stay interview outcome because headhunters are calling into your company to take your talent. In this case the manager likely went to his or her manager and maybe to HR to develop a plan that included course work, shadowing, mentoring, coaching, and other developmental opportunities.

Managers who conduct stay interviews learn that sometimes buying time is a helpful tactic. Whereas many requests can be resolved in the initial meeting, others require careful consideration and planning. Rather than provide shallow solutions on the spot, these managers instead ask, listen, and probe to learn precisely what the employee needs to engage and stay. They conclude the meeting by summarizing their understanding and scheduling a second meeting a week or so later. Then they reread their notes for a day or two and perhaps ask for help from others. Mostly they recognize that one size never fits all and instead develop solutions that come as close as possible to meeting the ideal outcome for the employee.

Do Stay Interviews Actually Improve Retention?

Our clients that have applied stay interviews have seen turnover drop by more than 30 percent for nurses and by 50 percent in call centers—in the first year. These improvements have been so consistent that we guarantee clients from all industries their turnover will fall by at least 20 percent in the first year or we return their money.

We know that leaders at all levels must participate, they all must feel the drive to retain their teams, and they all must be trained to probe and then develop the right, customized stay plans for each employee.

Think about other solutions you have purchased like engagement surveys, exit surveys, career planning, compensation, or management training on any level. Have any of them guaranteed turnover will fall or they refund your money? Think, too, about the time your managers spend with other "solutions" that not only bring no guarantees but do not change your numbers.

Stay Interviews versus Engagement and Exit Surveys

I said earlier that a major engagement survey shortcoming is they lead to one-size-fits-all programs rather than to individual solutions. But one positive outcome of engagement surveys is that they identify the things about your company and your jobs that concern employees the most. It makes sense, then, to add a few questions to your stay interviews that reflect these areas, so managers can probe to learn more about what concerns employees and provide real fixes.

Many of our clients have discontinued their exit surveys because when done correctly, stay interviews tell us who might leave and why. Stay interviews eliminate the quits for which we now say, "If only I knew that was important." Ideally quits now happen either because we cannot address a pressing need or because employees quit for personal reasons beyond our control.

No Sacred Cows

Put yourself in the shoes of a manager. We have now told you that you are responsible for your talent, that you have engagement and retention goals you must achieve, and that reports will tell us if you do. We have also said that this stay interview tool will help you achieve your goals.

Managers, then, know they must solve employees' issues to the best of their abilities. Savvy ones will go upstream with complex issues as a way of self-protection, saying to their managers and beyond, "If you want me to achieve my goals, I need your help to solve this employee's request."

This is a good thing. We know that first-line supervisors have the strongest impact on how much employees apply themselves and how long they stay. Real solutions, then, the most effective ones, must start at the bottom and then go up. As pressure rises bottom-up regarding topics such as schedules or work conditions, executives make policy improvements. And they are more likely to do so when they hear real-world stories about top performers than they are from engagement or exit survey results.

Let's close this chapter with a quote from Mary Murcott, who is president of an outsourcing call center company named Dialog Direct. After I trained Mary's managers to conduct stay interviews, Mary stepped to the front of the room and said the following with no notes in hand:

> I sat in the back of the room this morning and couldn't help but think about the ways we've been taught to think about our employees compared to how we think about our customers. We all know that "Customer Management 101" says never assume you know what your customers think so you need to ask them—that silence from customers is never good news. So in restaurants and other businesses you see executives approach customers and ask their opinions of the services they just received.

> But this is different than how we treat employees. We build walls between us and them by asking opinions in anonymous surveys which protects us from looking in their eyes and hearing their words. Maybe down deep we have a fear that they will ask for something and we'll have to say no. Or maybe they'll ask for something that you think they deserve but don't have the authority to give them.

> We can't become a great company unless we ask, listen, and then consider every reasonable request. So my commitment to you is that our top team and I will listen to any idea you hear that you think has merit, either for all employees or just for one. You know that our most important goal is to run a profitable business for our shareholders so we cannot say yes to every request. But our employees know this too, and I don't think they will ask for impossible things.

Let's declare that the game is over for sacred cows regarding pay, schedules, benefits, and all other subjects we usually run away from. Above all else, let's be courageous and reasonable, and I am certain our employees will be reasonable, too.[9]

Table 6.1.

Comparative Processes	Sales	Service	Engagement and Retention
3. Train and provide tools	Product training, sales training, collateral sales materials, administrative tools and training to use them	Product training, service training, administrative tools and training to use them	Leaders conduct stay interviews as a process, on schedule, and develop stay plans for each employee; all compensation, benefits, training, and programs work better then.

5 Questions/Suggestions for You and Your C-Suite Executives to Overcome HR's Greatest Challenge

1. Reread the section on overcoming stay interview objections and choose the objection you are most likely to hear. Then plan your response.

NOTES: _____

_____

_____

_____

_____

2. If your C-suite executives are reluctant to support stay interviews, educate them on the value of increased engagement and retention with data from this book and the heavy roles managers play to achieve these goals. Ask them what one better thing managers have to do with their time than engage and retain their teams.

NOTES: _____

_____

_____

_____

_____

3. Think through the processes that absorb your managers' time for little value in return. These might include administrative work, daylong meetings, midyear performance reviews, or engagement or retention solutions that involve activities but no tracking toward desired outcomes. Then identify who you must influence to eliminate these processes and do so.

NOTES: _____

_____

_____

_____

_____

4. Which manager jobs in your company have too many direct reports for managers to do stay interviews effectively? Consider ways this structure affects profitability in ways beyond stay interviews as well and then recommend a solution. Include the dollar values for engagement and retention as reasons to make these changes.

NOTES: _____

_____

_____

_____

_____

5. List the major "sacred cows" that reduce engagement and retention in your company that up until now have been untouchable. Share these with your C-suite executives, and ask for their feedback and their recommendations for change.

NOTES: _____

_____

_____

_____

_____

Chapter 7.

Forecasting: The Lock-Down Engagement and Retention Tool

Comparative Processes	Sales	Service	Engagement and Retention
4. Forecast future performance	Sales executives use forecasts to reallocate resources and sometimes alert CEOs; sales managers use forecasts to motivate salespeople	Standards or goals are usually the forecast unless obstacles require interim steps to achieve service goals	Forecasts rarely occur

Let us break new ground and introduce forecasting as an innovative, lock-down, results-driving tool to improve engagement and retention.

Executive level HR professionals who work in publicly traded companies sit through many sessions where CEOs, CFOs, and sales executives establish forecasts, track progress against forecasts, and sometimes sweat out whether forecasts will be achieved. CFOs are especially adept at "creative accounting" to produce numbers that ultimately align closely to those reported previously to stock analysts. Analysts like predictability and reflect their likings when making buy recommendations to those who purchase stocks, and these purchasers ultimately determine the value of corporations. And the market value of corporations to some degree determines executives' pay.

At their best, forecasts cause people to predict and perform. Our interest is *performance* because the type of forecasting I will recommend has less value for its degree of accuracy than it has for causing supervisors to think, "My manager knows I committed to this forecast, so I better make it happen." My many years of teaching managers to forecast retention has convinced me without question that these forecasts become motivational tools for managers to step up their retention efforts. Academic research at Carnegie Mellon and other universities finds this to be true as well.[1]

The idea that managers forecast how long employees will stay was born in a conference room of a client technology company. This company struggled to find qualified workers and also to keep them for a full first year. To improve early turnover, we implemented stay interviews along with asking each manager to accept a goal to improve first-year retention. I suggested that we also ask managers to forecast whether each employee would reach his or her one-year anniversary after each stay interview, thinking that this would cause that manager to set off a help alarm if he or she believed first-year retention was in jeopardy. At that moment the top operations executive expanded my suggestion and insisted that from that day forward all managers would forecast retention for each employee, one by one, after each stay interview. Turnover then fell significantly, and retention forecasting was born.

We learned in Chapter 4 that CEOs want more data regarding retention. Might they have interest in learning who is forecasted to leave, the reasons why they might leave, their performance levels, and the actions being taken to keep them?

How Much Does Forecasting Drive Retention?

Although I cannot measure the impact of forecasting on its own because we apply it with other solutions that are noted in this book, forecasting has proven to be a perfect partner to both retention goals and stay interviews. The shorthand definition that comes to my mind for improving retention is:

Retention = Goals + Tools and Those Tools Become Processes

Forecasting, then, is a tool that must become a process, baked into the standard way your managers operate every day. It is a tactic, a solution, in that it drives positive behaviors and also sequences perfectly after managers understand they must achieve retention goals and then apply stay interviews as primary tools. Stay interviews then take on an added importance for managers as they now not only focus on learning actions they can take to improve engagement and retention but also know during the interview that they must learn the right information to commit to a forecast.

Leader Power Examples #16, #17, #18, and #19: How Much Do Leaders Affect Engagement?

Development Dimensions International (DDI) found that "engagement is strongly influenced by leader quality," that employees' engagement levels are considerably higher when workers' supervisors also had higher engagement levels, and that employees who report to highly engaged supervisors are less likely to indicate they may leave the organization within a year.[2]

The U.S. Merit Systems Protection Board found that 87 percent of engaged employees agreed that their supervisors had good management skills. Of the employees who were not engaged, just 13.7 percent agreed their supervisors had good management skills.[3]

The American Society for Training and Development (now the Association for Talent Development) found that just 15 percent of respondents agree to a high or very high extent that their leaders are skilled at engaging the workforce, concluding "the bottom line is that many leaders and managers need considerably better engagement-building skills than they currently have."[4]

And knowing the strong link between disengagement and high turnover, the Saratoga Institute found poor leadership causes over 60 percent of all employee turnover. Its study covered more than 19,000 employees across 17 industry groups and found the main reasons employees leave are because they are not recognized or are not coached by their supervisors.[5]

Retention Forecasting Nuts and Bolts

We found that retention forecasting must be presented to managers in a way that is both easy so they make only one decision and colorful so we can produce eye-grabbing reports. The method we established is this:

» Code the employee as green if you forecast he or she will stay at the organization for one year or more.

» Code the employee as yellow if you forecast he or she will stay 6 to 12 months.

» Code the employee as red if you forecast he or she will stay less than 6 months.

After several tries we have learned to keep it simple. Do not look too far out and do not provide criteria for managers to use when making their decisions; just ask them to make a decision. They should make a decision based on everything they learned in their just-completed stay interviews and on any other information they know. Managers need to look at possible turnover from both sides, whether the employee will quit or will be fired.

Reports, then, can spotlight trouble spots according to criteria that matter most. We report forecasted turnover by performance, by job such as software engineers, by length of service to attack early turnover, by gender or race for affirmative action, and of course by each individual manager. Forecasts can be entered into an unused field in your HR information system (HRIS) system or in a separate Excel spreadsheet to which you can import other employee information. Table 7.1 illustrates one type of report we have used with clients.

Table 7.1. Retention Forecast "HeatMap"

Leader: Rodriguez	Performance Rating: 5 High, 1 Low	Green 1+ Years	Yellow 6-12 Months	Red 0-6 Months	Retention Plan
Kim Johnson	4	▨			Provide mentor for her to learn organizing skills
Burt Brown	5			■	Develop skills for possible promotion to a management position
Cindy Stone	3	▨			Pleased with current role and circumstance
Ralph Jimenez	2		▨		Coaching for performance

This was an original report for a software company that its top executive named the "heatmap." That executive brings this report monthly to his executive meeting to talk through yellows and reds, the action plans to retain them, and the contingency plans if the company loses them. The degree of top-level concern is based on the employee's performance, of course. Names have been changed.

Michelle Rodriguez is the department manager, and included on the heatmap are four direct reports:

» Kim Johnson is an above-average performer, a 4 with 5 being most high and, based on her stay interview, Rodriguez has forecasted that Kim will remain with the company for at least another year. She notes that Kim wants to learn new skills and has provided a mentor to coach her to improve her organizing skills.

» Burt Brown is Rodriguez's top performer, and Rodriguez has unearthed a major problem during Burt's stay interview. Burt has disclosed that he works too many hours, has earned his stripes, continues to receive headhunter calls, and will seek a management position either in this company or another one. Rodriguez has consulted with her management and HR to present a management development solution to Burt to qualify him for a promotion. Burt has accepted the learning opportunity with a "we'll see" approach. Rodriguez discreetly questions whether Burt is right for management but proceeds with the plan. So for now, Rodriguez has coded Burt "red," meaning that Burt could be gone within six months. Should Bert learn all the required skills and qualify to be moved into a management position, Rodriguez will move Bert's retention code to green.

» Cindy Stone is steady. She likes what she does, has no major issues with Rodriguez or the company, and Rodriguez was unable to learn any circumstance that could cause Cindy to leave.

» Ralph Jimenez is a low performer. Ralph must improve his basic job performance, or he will be terminated. Rodriguez is optimistic enough to code Ralph as yellow rather than as red but recognizes she might lose Ralph if Ralph fails to improve or becomes frustrated with possibly being a misfit for his job.

The role for Rodriguez and for all managers is clear: Forecast employees as best you can based on stay interview results and other knowledge, and then move employees from red to yellow to green based on successful implementations of each employee's stay plan. And always address and if necessary terminate poor performers. Managers can change forecasts any time, with or without conducting another stay interview.

How Accurately Can Managers Forecast Retention?

By definition, 50 percent of all doctors graduated in the bottom half of their classes. I say this tongue-in-cheek because it is way too easy to put people into a group and assume they can all do things equally well.

We learned in Chapter 6 that the most important skill a manager can have to improve engagement and retention is to build trust. Without building trust, all aspects of leadership fly out the window. This is true for stay interviews, too, as managers who have developed trust will gain better information and make better forecasts.

Obstacles to accurate forecasting are (a) lack of employee disclosure and (b) surprises. Leaders who build trust and also probe effectively have the best chance to forecast accurately because they will learn every possible job and life circumstance the employee is willing to share. Leaders who do not build trust and compound their positions by accepting shallow stay interview answers usually forecast optimistically, heavy on greens. Recall, too, that some turnover is completely out of managers' control for reasons neither they nor the employee see coming, such as an aging parent needing the employee to relocate back to his or her hometown.

This forecasting is not designed to be scientific. Let's instead label it as precautionary and as a motivating, behavior-improving accountability tool for managers. Our objective is for managers to accept retention goals, conduct effective stay interviews, forecast how long each employee will stay, and then leverage their newly found knowledge to take actions that lead to legitimate green forecasts and improve retention.

My experience has made clear that the best managers have the most accurate forecasts and that the worst have the least accurate. Forecasts, then, become another tool for manager evaluation. The best managers are the most connected with their teams, gain the most information about each member by building relationships daily, and combine that knowledge with each employee's performance and other signals that reach their attuned antennae to deliver strong insights into each employee's inner thoughts. Substandard managers, on the other hand, remain in the dark and will see forecasting as another "to do." And many managers are in the middle who will hopefully learn lessons from stay interviews and unanticipated exits that will cause them to grow their forecasting skills.

Said another way, the goal is not to forecast with 100 percent accuracy. The goal is to identify employees at risk of leaving and also motivate managers to cut employee turnover.

Retention Forecasting Is a Trendy Tool

As the U.S. spun out of its terrible recession, we learned STEM (science, technology, engineering, and mathematics) workers and others were in short supply, and a few vendors and companies implemented data-driven methods to forecast turnover. The process makes sense in that if you put certain data into a formula, you can likely predict which areas will have higher future turnover. Factors like past turnover, specific unemployment data, employees' lengths of service, and performance come to mind as being possibly included.

Although these methods are being touted as both new and helpful, *I wonder what solutions these vendors or companies will implement to cut turnover once they have their data.* Will they conduct engagement surveys and then implement HR-driven programs to fix recognition, communication, and career development, the same ineffective methods of the past? Or will they approach leaders of these teams to set retention goals, provide tools such as stay interviews, and ask them to forecast employee turnover—and then be accountable for all?

Gaining data for future turnover possibilities is a good thing. The goal, though, is bigger—to improve retention. Connecting new-found data to the wrong historical solutions will lead to the same ineffective results.

Additional Retention Forecast Reports

A hospital client was rightly concerned about losing nurses in their first two years. This rural hospital is located such that new nurses can drive a few hours in several directions to relocate to a major-city hospital, and it is commonly known that these major-city hospitals crave nurses with two years of experience. They also typically offer more money and a more active, urban lifestyle. The director of nursing implemented stay interviews and required managers to conduct them at 90 and 180 days for new hires. We structured a report for him that looked like Table 7.2.

Table 7.2. Forecasted Retention by Length of Service

Forecasted Retention/ Length of Service	0-6 months (%)	6-12 months (%)	12-18 months (%)	18-24 months (%)
Green, 1 year +	67	62	71	74
Yellow, 6-12 months	23	26	20	21
Red, 0-6 months	10	12	9	5
Total	100	100	100	100

The data tracked closely to actual retention results, with some managers of course forecasting more accurately than others. A close look shows that getting new nurses to their first anniversaries correlated with an increase in optimism to retain them.

Most executives want to see forecasted turnover by performance. This report is standard in our package and presents turnover likelihood by performance rating, and can be presented for entire organizations, for departments, or by job (see Table 7.3).

Table 7.3. Forecasted Retention/Performance Rating

	Rating				
	5 (%)	4 (%)	3 (%)	2 (%)	1 (%)
	Highest		Middle		Lowest
Green, 1 year +	84	77	54	5	2
Yellow, 6-12 months	11	8	25	47	46
Red, 0-6 months	5	15	21	48	52
Total	100	100	100	100	100

Studying these data closely, it appears this organization has sent a clear, reasonable message to managers that addressing poor performance is more important than achieving retention goals. There is belief that a few substandard performers will be onboard in 12 months, and all other substandard performers are projected to be gone.

We have designed additional reports for organizations that encompass all demographics. Those organizations that identify top performers or high potentials by name receive reports that detail each named employee's retention projection and detailed retention action plan.

This underscores another strong advantage stay interviews bring over engagement surveys. Each individual employee's stay plan and forecast is available to top management by name because companies are not encumbered by batched data and employee anonymity. And there is no pretense of confidentiality. All stay plans and forecasts are available to each employee's direct supervisor and those above that supervisor so specific actions can be taken to resolve important retention and engagement issues.

Forecasting Employee's Engagement Scores

Forecasting retention can be easily reconciled in that we will eventually know how long each employee stays. Forecasting engagement is more difficult because engagement results are anonymous and individual results are buried in department data.

Let's explore two ways we can forecast engagement. This first way is to ask each manager to forecast his or her next retention score against the most recent one, as in "I scored a 28 this time, and next time I'll score a 29."

Though this method is easy to administer, it likely leads to selection of an arbitrary number, one that managers will quietly discuss with each other to learn what degree of improvement is acceptable. Worse, it causes managers to see their teams as packs rather than as collections of individual people, and the resulting group focus can switch the managers' thinking toward implementing group programs. Their line of sight becomes, "To improve by two points I need to raise that communication score. We'll have more meetings." This first way fails to inspire the right behaviors.

So let me recommend the second way, which is to ask managers after each stay interview to forecast if that specific employee will score in the top box on the next engagement survey. And make the question closed-ended, requiring the manager to check "yes" or "no."

Let's harken back to Chapter 1 where we learned that top-box performers contribute far more productivity than those in the middle box. The lesson here is that only the top box counts. Your survey company might label the middle box as "partly engaged" or some other term that implies a degree of engagement, but the clear expectation we must convey to managers is to lead as many employees as they can to score in the top box.

I recommended in Chapter 2 that you ask your survey company to break out your top-box score for your organization and for each department, regardless of what name they assign to the middle box. Then after each survey you will be able to compare the percentage of employees each manager forecasts to score in the top box to those that actually do.

While we cannot know if the precise employees scored in the top box as forecasted because of confidentiality, we have nonetheless motivated each manager to forecast and then achieve their forecasts. This is a good thing.

This might seem like a fuzzy assignment to managers the first time around: "How can we predict how employees will fill out a questionnaire?" and "What can I possibly do to encourage them to work harder when we're so understaffed?" But after one round of reporting and comparison to forecasts, they will come to understand that they are responsible for engaging their talent, and in some cases they will raise standards and ultimately take action against those who cannot be moved to perform at their best. And their attention to detail in stay interviews will also increase.

Forecasts as the Antidote to Infrequent Reports

One obstacle to moving engagement and retention into the top-5 metric status is infrequent reporting. Turnover is reported at best monthly, and engagement is typically reported once per year or even less frequently. One solution with engagement is to conduct quarterly surveys as recommended in Chapter 5, but even quarterly or monthly cannot compete with the daily data that cross CEOs' screens and dominate their attention.

To some degree forecasts fill this gap. Recall that even though managers must enter a retention forecast after each stay interview, they can change that forecast at any time. They should have the identical change-when-it-is-right opportunity for forecasting whether or not each employee will score top-box on the next engagement survey, too. These data can then be presented to executives with periodic updates by each manager so executives can track each employee's forecast against performance ... and also track each manager's effectiveness at forecasting each employee's levels of engagement.

Let's close our forecasting discussion by updating our comparative processes in Table 7.4. We will make major leaps to improve engagement and retention by asking managers to forecast their successes, and then as you will see in Chapter 8, hold them accountable to both their engagement and retention goals and their forecasts.

Table 7.4.

Comparative Processes	Sales	Service	Engagement and Retention`
4. Forecast future performance	Sales executives use forecasts to reallocate resources and sometimes alert CEOs; sales managers use forecasts to motivate salespeople	Standards or goals are usually the forecast unless obstacles require interim steps to achieve service goals	Forecast individual employee retention and engagement after each stay interview and update as appropriate.

5 Questions/Suggestions for You and Your C-Suite Executives to Overcome HR's Greatest Challenges

1. To gain experience and confidence, pilot these forecasting methods in HR first. Gather your managers and ask them to provide forecasts for retention and top-box engagement for each employee, even if they have not yet conducted stay interviews with their employees. Ask them to bring these forecasts to your next one-on-one meeting, so you can learn their thinking on reasons for forecasts and plans to improve the results.

NOTES: _____

_____

_____

_____

_____

2. Ask if you can be on the agenda for a meeting of middle managers. In the meeting, ask these managers to spontaneously and privately forecast how long each of their employees will stay using the red/

yellow/green method included here. After they have completed this assignment, ask them if they have already considered specific actions they will take to improve retention based on this exercise.

NOTES: _____

_____

_____

_____

_____

3. Report to your C-suite team that you have discovered a method to forecast how long each employee will stay and also how he or she will perform on the next engagement survey. Show them sample reports you can develop based on these data to stimulate their interest and support.

NOTES: _____

_____

_____

_____

_____

4. Executives will support your asking managers to forecast whether employees will score in the top box of your next engagement survey only if they fully understand the degree to which top-box performers drive productivity. If you have not already, share with them the data in Chapter 1 to gain their support for asking managers to make this forecast for each employee.

NOTES: _____

_____

_____

_____

_____

5. If you meet resistance from your top team to implement either retention or engagement forecasting across your company, seek out one savvy executive who manages a substantial team and pilot this forecasting with those team members. Then ask that executive to share forecasting's ultimate impact on engagement and retention with the remainder of the top team to gain companywide support.

NOTES: _____

_____

_____

_____

_____

Chapter 8.
Real Accountability

Comparative Processes	Sales	Service	Engagement and Retention
5. Holds employees accountable to goals	Reports issued daily in most organizations; consequences vary with extremes from large bonuses to getting fired	Reports issued daily in most organizations; poor customer service can lead to loss of job	Tracking occurs but few meaningful consequences for managers or for HR

Our engagement and retention solution pattern is becoming clear:

» Convert engagement and retention to dollars to make them top-5 metrics.
» Inspire executives to establish engagement and retention goals.
» Implement stay interviews as the primary engagement and retention tool.
» Forecast each individual employee's engagement and retention based on stay interview results.

And now we hit the major bump in the road because all is naught without accountability. If you cannot influence your executives to hold leaders at all levels accountable, your engagement and retention initiative will suddenly become a one-cycle wonder.

Where Is Engagement and Retention Accountability Today?

A good place to start this discussion is to examine your organization's engagement and retention accountabilities today. I recommended four specific metrics for accountability in Chapter 5, and they are listed in Table 8.1. You might have other metrics you want to include, too. Please review and possibly adjust these metrics, add your own in the extra row provided if you have additional ones, and then pencil in your current accountabilities as well as consequences.

Table 8.1. The Engagement and Retention Goal-Setting Chart

Metric	Recommended Goal-Setting Methodology	Who Is Accountable?	How Is Their Performance Reported?	How Frequently Is Their Performance Reported?	What Consequences Do They Face, Positive or Negative?
Engagement	Continuous annual 20% increase of top-box score				
All Turnover	20% annual decrease until annual turnover is 10% or less				
First-Year Turnover	20% annual decrease until first-year turnover is 5% or less				
High Performers	Retain 95% each year				
Additional Metrics					

The accountabilities you have detailed likely become good evidence for the need to change. As we move forward, consider presenting your findings to your C-suite team and asking if any of them disagree. Spreading awareness of your current degree of accountability can be crucial to achieving *greater* accountability, especially if current accountability is lacking.

Cannon-Fire from Above and Below

So why might you need these data to convince your top team? Because holding managers at all levels accountable for engagement and retention is new for many executives and might still go against the grain of some of your executives' beliefs. It is logical, it is common sense, to see that managers must produce work through their teams, so they therefore must engage and retain their teams to perform their jobs successfully. But common sense is not always common practice.

Establishing goals implies accountability, but *administering* accountability requires another level of leadership effectiveness.

Some managers will think similarly as in, "I know I had goals, but was it really important that I achieved them?" In fairness, why should they believe things have really changed until things really *do* change?

We conduct focus groups with our clients' employees and supervisors, and the typical outcomes tell how supervisors view their roles with retention. We ask employees on a 1-to-10 scale with 10 being high, "How important is your immediate supervisor in your decisions to stay or leave?" The most common answer is 7 or 8. Then we ask supervisors on a 1-to-10 scale with 10 being high, "How important are you in your employees' decisions to stay or leave?" The most common answer is 3 or 4.

The consistent lesson is that many supervisors at all levels vastly underestimate their power to engage and retain their teams. They assign too much value to what they cannot change such as pay, sometimes schedules, and other conditions that they believe matter more than their own influence. So enforcing accountability will sound a few self-defense alarms within the top-to-bottom management team.

My Early Introduction to the Power of Accountability

When I was an HR executive, our CEO had come up through the marketing ranks and saw profitability through the lens of great service. He also believed exceptional service was the result of great training, and his comments over the years indicated he thought training could fix any offbeat behaviors.

One day he called me into his office to tell me that the employees at his grocery store were the very best and that I should go there to learn the details of their customer service training. Following his request, I went to the store later that week, purchased a few items, and proceeded to check out. There I was greeted by a smiling woman who made exceptional eye contact and welcomed me to the store. I asked what training she received to be so effective, and she said, "We're really not trained this way, sir. Our manager tells us to smile, say a greeting, and act pleased to be here. We've seen others get fired for not doing this, so believe me, sir, we do it."

There went my hopes for increasing the training budget. And I learned that accountability is far less expensive.

Again, Sales and Service Lead Us to Solutions

We have become smarter by borrowing process steps from sales and service, so let's do the same for accountability. My experience in working with most industries and across six continents has taught me that sales managers coach substandard salespeople this way:

- » They do not panic when salespeople get off to slow starts; instead they coach.
- » When salespeople need additional training in product knowledge or sales skills, the sales managers provide it via a class, assigning a mentor, or coaching them one-on-one.
- » When salespeople have difficulty closing sales, the sales managers tag along, observe, and provide feedback.

» When salespeople lose key accounts, managers investigate to learn whether the loss was the fault of the salesperson or was beyond his or her control, such as a key client who is struggling financially and can no longer afford your service or a new CEO bringing in your competitor as his or her favorite provider.
» When salespeople across the board struggle, their managers look first for problems with products or marketing.
» When salespeople have multiple opportunities to succeed, and a full array of coaching does not help them, their managers move them out of their sales roles and likely fire them.

The important point is that supervisors have been chosen for the skills they bring, and the core belief is they are qualified to engage and retain their teams. Some need extra help to achieve their goals. And ultimately a few lack the talent and will never achieve their goals. But this pattern is a far distance from saying, "You missed your goal, and you are fired." That is not the way performance management happens, and it is not the way it should happen with engagement and retention.

Yet the reality is that just as with sales and service, some leaders at all levels will fail to improve engagement and retention, lacking not only the skills but also the talent. And after coaching and having several chances to prove themselves, they must be moved out. Especially if they cannot build trust.

Leader Power Examples #20, #21, #22, and #23: Pay is not the Engagement and Retention Driver

Kenexa surveyed over 1,000 employees who had left organizations and asked about their fit with supervisors as well as their satisfaction with pay, benefits, learning, development, and advancement. In all instances, employees' opinions were "mediated," or influenced by relationships these employees had with their supervisors. The study concluded by saying, "Offering a higher salary or developmental/advancement opportunities may not be enough to retain employees."

Said another way, poor supervisors drag down employees' opinions about all aspects of their employees' work experience. The next time you hear employees complain about pay, they might instead be complaining about their bosses.[1]

Yahoo found more than 70 percent of employees surveyed said they were open to landing a new job in the coming year, and the primary reason was disliking the way their bosses performed their jobs. Finding a job that paid more money was not nearly as important as avoiding a bad boss. When asked if they agree with the statement "People don't leave companies, they leave managers," over half said yes.[2]

In a survey of 1,000 U.S. executives, 65 percent of respondents said a better boss would make them happy. Only 35 percent said a pay raise will do the same thing.[3]

And in the broadest of all studies, Gallup surveyed over 1 million employees from a broad range of industries, companies, and countries and drew these conclusions:

> Our research yielded many discoveries but the most powerful was this: Talented employees need great managers. The talented employee may join a company because of its charismatic leaders, its generous benefits, and its world-class training programs, but how long that employee stays and how productive he is while he is there is determined by his relationship with his immediate supervisor.
>
> Gallup went on to say: "We discovered that the manager—not pay, benefits, perks, or a charismatic corporate leader—was the critical player in building a strong workplace."[4]

So let us reintroduce the four goals provided in Chapter 5 and present methods to coach all those who fail to meet them. Your goals of course might be different, but the scenarios presented here will still apply. These are just some of the coaching questions that must be posed to ensure all efforts are made to maximize goal achievement. I will address the first two goals together because their coaching questions are the same as shown in Table 8.2.

First Goal: Increase Engagement with Continual Annual 20% Increase in Top-Box Score

Second Goal: Decrease All Turnover 20% Annually Until Turnover Is 10% or Less

Table 8.2. The Engagement and Retention Goal-Setting Chart

Metric	Recommended Goal-Setting Methodology	CEO	Direct Supervisors and All Managers above Them Including C-suite Executives	Executive-level HR	HR Recruiters	Trainers
Engagement	Continuous annual 20% increase of top-box score	Yes	Yes	Yes	No	No
All Turnover	20% annual decrease until annual turnover is 10% or less	Yes	Yes	Yes	No	No

» **For the CEO:** Do I conduct stay interviews effectively with my direct reports to model the right way for them and those who report to them? Do I exhibit the right behaviors to earn trust every day with every employee in my company? Am I holding my direct reports accountable for engagement throughout their departments in meaningful ways? Are there major, overarching issues across our company that obstruct managers from being able to fully engage their teams, such as rumors or the reality of being acquired, shutting down, or laying workers off? If yes, what steps can I take to minimize fear about these circumstances? Are there members of my executive team who are poisoning the company with their distrustful behaviors? Is my push for continual improvement too strong, wearing out our team and therefore making our organization a difficult place to work? Am I too "old school" regarding flexible schedules or other policies that affect employees in a consistently negative way? Might my increased visibility send the messages that I care and that our company is sound? Or might my presence reflect my being stern, uncaring, and even narcissistic? Have I been needlessly cheap about purchasing new equipment that increases productivity and provides an emotional lift? Is our pay plan driving the wrong behaviors?

» **For direct supervisors and all managers above them, including C-suite executives**: Do I conduct stay interviews effectively and on time? Do I listen carefully, probe deeply, and take good notes to ensure I am getting all the data I can from each stay interview? Do the stay plans I build address the right issues for each of my direct reports? Do I fulfill my obligations for each stay plan? Do I follow up months later to ensure my plan with each direct report is on track, even though I have fulfilled my initial obligations? Do I interact with my direct reports in ways that disclose my genuine self to give them a chance to know me and like me? Do I consistently earn their trust and apologize when I fail to do so? Do I support company policies, so all know I am part of the total team?

If I manage other managers, do I ask about their stay interviews and action plans and follow up to ensure they are keeping their obligations to the fullest? Do I ask what specific steps they will take with each employee whom they forecast to achieve top-box engagement status? Do I ask why they do not forecast other employees to achieve top-box status and coach them to supervise those employees more effectively?

» **For the executive HR professional:** Do I need to coach the CEO to hold leaders accountable for engagement and retention? Or to improve communications, agree to new policies, approve new expenditures, or make other changes to improve overall engagement? Might another C-suite executive behave in negative ways that greatly influences engagement for a large number of employees, and might I need to address this directly with that executive or the CEO? Are some of our policies outdated or just wrong so that I must have courage to fix them? Are ineffective employees slipping through the new-hire gate, so I must address my team and our processes to improve the situation? Are some midmanagers or first-line supervisors consistently breaking trust with their teams so that I must sound an alarm at the top to improve them or remove them? Are there one or more hotspot departments or locations where rumors are rampant and negativity is dominant?

Third Goal: Decrease First-Year Turnover 20% Annually Until First-Year Turnover is No More Than 5%

Table 8.3. The Engagement and Retention Goal-Setting Chart

Metric	Recom-mended Goal-Setting Methodology	CEO	Direct Supervisors and All Managers above Them Including C-suite Executives	Executive-level HR	HR Recruiters	Trainers
First-Year Turnover	20% an-nual decrease until first-year turnover is 10% or less	Yes	Yes	Yes	Yes	Yes

» **For the CEO:** Are the right processes in place to hire the right people and retain them in their first years? Have I reinforced accountabilities for those who have them? Do reports tell me every bit of data I need to know to scrutinize this issue and recommend targeted areas for improvement? Have we rightly measured the cost of first-year turnover and communicated it to those who have the most impact? Are we losing people because they are a poor fit or because our managers are failing to keep them?

» **For direct supervisors and all managers above them including C-suite executives:** Am I conducting at least two stay interviews for new hires and doing them on schedule? Am I listening, probing, and acting on what I hear? Do new hires feel socially welcome? Are they connecting with others and, if not, how can I help? Can I recommend a fine-tune revision to the hiring process that better measures a complex skill? Are my own interviewing skills sharp enough? Is there another manager who is better and who might coach me or team-interview with me? Can I redirect our recruiters to screen some skills or characteristics out and others in? Do I spend enough one-on-one time with new hires, either coaching them or getting to know them? Do I behave like someone they want to open up to and trust? Should I select one or two who appear to be forthright and ask how I can be a better supervisor to new hires?

If I manage other managers, do they talk to me about stay interview specifics, or must I pull the details out of them? Do the managers conduct stay interviews with new hires? Do they block time on their calendars to coach new hires? Do they seem aware that they must connect socially with new hires and others on the team to put the employees at ease and to make them want to stay here, or do the managers focus on performance only? Do the managers hire well, or do they choose people who are like them or maybe people they can dominate? Are they afraid to hire smart people?

» **For the executive HR professional:** Are stay interviews being completed on time? Do stay plans contain enough details? Is there evidence stay plans are being fulfilled? Are retention forecasts being completed and recorded? Are there consistent tipping points by job that indicate how long we must retain employees until they tend to stay longer? Do we have the best methods in place to attract the best candidates? Are our hiring processes the absolute best they can be? Are our recruiters top-notch, the best I have ever worked with? Do our recruiters fully understand our jobs? Are recruiters attuned to the specific skill needs for the jobs, or do they leave skill assessment to the supervisors? Do we have the best assessments for the jobs we have? Is early turnover disproportionate among a few departments or supervisors, and if so, am I alerting their executives? Is our new-hire training the best it can be? Can I say for certain all who make hiring decisions have attended new-hire training? Does our onboarding program not only communicate company values and information but also inspire? Are our new-hire training programs designed and delivered flawlessly?

» **For HR recruiters:** When I rank-order my job skills, what am I worst at? Who can coach me to improve? Do I know the jobs I recruit for at least 80 percent as well as their supervisors do? Have I watched incumbents do all aspects of these jobs? Am I clear on why new hires fail in these jobs and also why they quit, so I can discern if applicants will turn over early? Will I take the heat to leave a job open rather than to refer a substandard candidate? Do I learn why my hires have left early to learn lessons and adjust my methods? Have I developed and applied realistic job previews to eliminate square pegs? Have I implemented a strong employee referral program to increase early retention?[5]

» **For trainers:** Is there perfect alignment between the skills required for the job and the skills I am teaching? Is my curriculum designed to give each trainee the best chance to learn these skills? Am I teaching the same skills that managers expect and reinforce on the job? Do my training methods keep trainees alert and involved, so they have the best chance to succeed? Am I a savvy observer of behavioral skills like punctuality, attendance, working with others, attention to detail, and respecting authority? Am I willing to retain trainees longer to ensure they have learned all the lessons? Do I graduate trainees whom I would not want to have reporting to me? Am I courageous enough to tell a supervisor no, that this trainee cannot cut it?

Fourth Goal: Retain 95% of High Performers/High Potentials Each Year

Table 8.4. The Engagement and Retention Goal-Setting Chart

Metric	Recommended Goal-Setting Methodology	CEO	Direct Supervisors and All Managers above Them Including C-suite Executives	Executive-level HR	HR Recruiters	Trainers
High Performers/High Potentials	Retain 95% each year	Yes	Yes	Yes	No	No

» **For CEOs:** Have we identified our high performers and high potentials by name? Do they make up no more than 25 percent of our total team so that we limit these lists to the very best? Have we appropriately disregarded performance ratings as criteria for inclusion? Can our processes for identification be tweaked to be better? Am I relying on unqualified managers to identify our top people? Are there managers whose roles call for supervising top performers who are not skilled to do so? Do I know the most valuable employees by name, and have I formed relationships with them?

» **For direct supervisors and all managers above them including C-suite executives:** Am I at my best when conducting stay interviews with top performers? Do I listen, probe, and develop stay plans that are mutually exciting for me and the employee? Do I always do what I say, to fulfill stay plans and more? Am I skilled to manage top performers? Can I coach effectively by both sharing feedback and giving autonomy? Can I accept different work methods if they produce great outcomes? Have I built relationships with top performers such that if they are considering leaving they will tell me? Do I believe I have all the authority I need to fulfill my top-performer retention goal? Who else can help me achieve this goal, above me or otherwise?

If I manage other managers, are these managers right fits to supervise our very best? Or do I need to move them into other roles? Have I reviewed their stay plans, and do I know they are fulfilling them? Do these managers ever break trust with me in such a way that I suspect they break trust with others?

» **For the executive HR professional:** Have I reviewed each stay plan for each top performer? Do these stay plans include solid developmental activities? Do I know for certain that each stay plan is being carried out? Where possible, have the CEO and other C-suite executives built individual relationships with our top performers? Do our top performers really know they are seen as top performers? Are we paying them the amount we think is right? Do we have poorly skilled supervisors managing top performers? Are we perfect, top to bottom, with hiring and grooming management trainees? Is there the right role model in the midmanagement ranks whom I need to lead hiring or training management trainees, and do I have the courage to get that person? Can I think of one top manager who connects strongly with each top performer, whether that manager directly manages the top performers or others? Are we leveraging that person to help?

The key message in this section is that when goals are missed, there is much investigation and soul-searching to be done. Our comparisons to sales and service become blurry here because tactical solutions for those have been in place for decades, whereas we are building them for engagement and retention from scratch. I believe engaging and retaining employees is also far more complicated because there are many more variables. Most sales and service relationships are short term, whereas many of us spend more time with our direct reports than we do with our families. Nowhere else in our lives do we deal with such strong issues related to authority, ego, competition, and sometimes financial survival. Work relationships can be very complex.

Sample Turnover Accountability Reports

Turnover is usually reported monthly, and I have suggested three separate goals: (a) for all turnover, (b) for first-year turnover, and (c) for high performers or high potentials. Table 8.5 is a sample report that captures all turnover and first-year turnover.

Table 8.5. Sample Turnover Report by Manager

Manager	Retention Goals	Year-to-Date Annualized Performance (%)	Year-to-Date Cost ($)
Ernie Hinderliter	All turnover, 15%	13	105,378
	1st-year turnover, 5%	3	31,254

Frank Joseph	All turnover, 15%	10	71,598
	1st-year turnover, 5%	5	49,560
Susan Seip	**All turnover, 15%**	**22**	**221,369**
	1st-year turnover, 5%	**11**	**88,321**

This report contains not only retention progress against goals but also turnover costs. Ernie Hinderliter is achieving his goals for both all turnover and first-year turnover, and the cost of his turnover is noted. Frank Joseph is achieving goals as well. Susan Seip, however, is behind on goals, and her costs are higher. On my company's client reports, Seip's information is bolded, and some of our clients report data for managers who are missing their goals in red or another font color. All turnover data are annualized to provide a clear comparison to the annual goals.

The high-performer/high-potential report can be designed in several ways as long as it includes at least the following:

» Names, positions, and managers of high performers who have left during the period.
» Retention forecast for employees who have left.
» Reason for the exit as best you can determine.
» Cost of each exit.
» Annualized projected turnover rate against goal by department and for your organization.

Table 8.6 is one of many ways these data can be presented.

Table 8.6. HiPo Turnover Manufacturing Division: Annualized Turnover Rate 3% vs. Goal 5%

Exiting Employee Name	Job	Manager	Forecast	Leave Reason	Cost ($)
Michael Derocco	Lathe tech	Joe Weimer	Green	New job better fit for skills	17,227
Scott Buchheit	Maintenance I	Roger Pynn	Green	Could not work for supervisor	15,679
Sherri Merbach	Supervisor II	Stan Latta	Yellow	Commute	32,445

Scot Lake	Assembler	Casey Corkery	Yellow	Spouse relocation	9,412
Mary Steele	Boilermaker	Kim DeZavala	Green	Return to school	11,478
Mackenzie Wade	Assistant plant manager	Roger Pynn	Green	Pay	37,804
Tony Bongiovanni	Maintenance II	Roger Pynn	Green	Schedule; preferred no weekend work	18,441
				TOTAL	142,486

Some would say the most useful data here are leave reasons, but on closer look we see that Roger Pynn has lost three high-performing employees. Notable, too, is that Pynn forecasted all as green, to stay at least one year. Leave reasons are "could not work for supervisor," "pay," and "schedule." One surmises that had Pynn conducted effective stay interviews and developed on-target stay plans, at least some of these exits could have been prevented. "Maybe they didn't trust Pynn" comes to mind given that one employee said he no longer wanted to work with him, and according to his forecasts, Pynn was surprised by all three exits. Digging into Pynn's stay plans for Mackenzie Wade and Tony Bongiovanni might uncover that Pynn was working to address their leave reasons, pay and schedule, or maybe not.

I would ask, too, if Pynn's manager had reviewed these stay plans and was also caught off-guard by these exits.

Reporting Engagement for Accountability

The majority of engagement reports are delivered by survey vendors, and they will have their own formats. How much they will reformat data for your company might depend on the size of your contract with them and whether you will pay additional fees. An ideal engagement report for accountability would contain the forecasted and actual increase in the percentages of top-box scores by organization, by department or division, and by manager.

What Consequences Should Be in Place for Missing Engagement and Retention Goals?

Because engagement and retention are now top-5 metrics, this question brings an easy answer. The same consequences should be put into place for missing engagement and retention goals as for missing sales and service goals. Investigate the causes, resharpen the manager's application of the processes, and follow the coaching tips earlier in this chapter—but ultimately managers must perform or stop being managers.

The same is true for executives, senior HR professionals, HR recruiters, and trainers. All must see accountability reports, receive coaching as needed, and ultimately perform. Compensation should also be affected similarly to sales and service. If executive bonuses contain possible dollars for sales and service, also include possible dollars for engagement and retention. Each manager's historical performance on engagement and retention should be front and center when considering who is promoted to larger management roles.

Chapter 1's purpose is to convince all readers that without question employee engagement and retention are essential for organizations to thrive and remain. No other metric should influence compensation more.

Manager-Supervisor Exit Interviews as One More Accountability Tool

Here is an idea to make exit interviews more effective. Regardless of whether you conduct traditional exit interviews, ask your managers to conduct an exit interview with the supervisors who report to them when those supervisors lose an employee. This installs another accountability event and also increases the opportunity for supervisors to learn lessons if lessons need to be learned. Retention forecasting adds strong additional data for investigation. Questions can include:

» Why do you think this employee left?

>>   What retention forecast did you assign to this employee?

>>   Did you see this exit coming?

>>   What actions did you take to prevent it?

>>   Did you fully carry out your stay plan with this employee?

>>   What lessons can you learn from this exit?

>>   Might there be other employees on your team who are planning to leave for the same reason?

If you conduct traditional exit surveys and believe the leave reasons they yield, compare the supervisors' reasons to those reasons to gain the best insight. We know one small-company CEO who will not sign off on a replacement requisition until both exit interviews occur and he learns all he can about why each employee has left.

This chapter asks that you make one giant leap, and we should not underestimate its importance. Let's close by updating our comparative process chart in Table 8.7.

Table 8.7. The Engagement and Retention Goal-Setting Chart

Comparative Processes	Sales	Service	Engagement and Retention
5. Holds employees accountable to goals	Reports issued daily in most organizations; consequences vary with extremes from large bonuses to getting fired	Reports issued daily in most organizations; poor customer service can lead to loss of job	Accountability, coaching, and consequences are in place

5 Questions/Suggestions for You and Your C-Suite Executives to Overcome HR's Greatest Challenge

1. Ask your C-suite executives if they can think of at least one manager in your company who cannot build trust with his or her team. Then ask what consequences that manager has faced as a result.

NOTES: _____

_____
_____
_____
_____

2. Ask your C-suite executives if they can think of any examples of managers being fired or displaced due to turnover or disengagement. If they give an example showing turnover or disengagement played a part in a manager's exit, ask if other performance issues contributed to that manager being removed. Is it possible that poor engagement or retention contributed to that manager's other sub-standard metrics as well?

NOTES: _____

_____
_____
_____
_____

3. Display your chart regarding engagement and retention accountability today to your C-suite team members and ask if they have the same or different opinions. Then ask if they believe they can drive their managers to better performance with the current levels of accountability.

NOTES: _____

_____
_____
_____
_____

4. What do you think is fair regarding holding HR accountable for engagement and retention? Regardless of the recommendations here, what do think is right for yourself and your team?

NOTES: _____

_____

_____

_____

5. Much of this chapter presents coaching recommendations for CEOs, executive-level HR professionals, and others on the leadership team who fail to make their engagement and retention goals. Reread these tips and underline the ones that you think will be most relevant for the noted employees in your organization.

NOTES: _____

_____

_____

_____

_____

Chapter 9.

Innovation from 10,000 Feet

"Imagination is more important than knowledge. Knowledge is limited. Imagination encircles the world."

—Albert Einstein

Let's first review our work in a few words:

  » Chapter 1 demonstrated that engagement and retention bring such high dollar values that they should be reported as top-5 metrics.

  » Chapter 2 supported that exit and engagement surveys, two of our primary tools, are permanently broken in their current forms.

  » Chapter 3 then opened our eyes to a winning approach, to improve engagement and retention with similar processes that our CEOs use to accelerate sales and service.

  » Then Chapters 4 through 8 detailed the five principal processes for that solution, which are (1) convert turnover percentages and survey scores to dollars, (2) establish improvement goals at the organizational and leader levels, (3) equip leaders to conduct stay interviews, (4) ask leaders for forecast engagement and retention for each individual employee, and (5) hold leaders accountable for their goals and forecasting.

The resulting flow chart that depicts our new-found processes is seen in Figure 9.1.

Figure 9.1 The Business-Driven Engagement and Retention Flow Chart

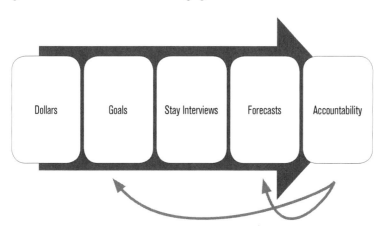

| Dollars | Goals | Stay Interviews | Forecasts | Accountability |

And our final, detailed process chart that compares our new processes to sales and service is demonstrated in Table 9.1.

Table 9.1.

Comparative Processes	Sales	Service	Current Engagement and Retention Processes	New Engagement and Retention Processes
1. Convert to dollars	Margins: "This product brings a 22% margin, which results in $4,000 for each sale going right to the bottom line"	Correlations: "For each 2% improvement in our service score, our revenues increase by $124,000"	Results reported in percentages and scores with no correlations to dollars; sometimes include comparisons to benchmarks	Results reported in dollars or correlations to propel engagement and retention to top-5 metrics
2. Establish goals	Essential for revenue generation and defined for total company, sales managers, and sales employees; goals are increased year to year and sometimes quarter to quarter	Drive additional business from current customers and referrals; defined for total company, service managers, and service employees	Most times retention goals either are not set at all or are set for the total organization; engagement goals are rarely established, and past scores and benchmarks serve as standards without specific improvement objectives	Engagement and retention goals are established for leaders at all levels and in some cases for HR too

3. Train and provide tools	Product training, sales training, collateral sales materials, administrative tools and training to use them	Product training, service training, administrative tools and training to use them	Compensation, benefits, management and supervisory training, surveys, employee programs	Leaders conduct stay interviews as a process, on schedule, and develop stay plans for each employee; all comp, benefits, training, and programs work better then.
4. Forecast future performance	Sales executives use forecasts to reallocate resources and sometimes alert CEOs; sales managers use forecasts to motivate salespeople	Standards or goals are usually the forecast unless obstacles require interim steps to achieve service goals	Forecasts rarely occur	Forecast individual employee retention and engagement after each stay interview and update as appropriate.
5. Hold employees accountable to goals	Reports issued daily in most organizations; consequences vary with extremes from large bonuses to getting fired	Reports issued daily in most organizations; poor customer service can lead to loss of job	Tracking occurs but few meaningful consequences for managers or for HR	Accountability, coaching, and consequences are in place

The model and our process chart display information on a strategic level, from high up, but contained throughout these chapters are several innovative tactics that merits our attention, such as:

» Inviting your CFO to measure turnover costs and engagement value in dollars with unique formulas to make these resulting dollar amounts more believable.

» Conducting correlative studies to learn which engagement survey items drive engagement and retention.

» Asking your engagement survey provider to retool reports, so you can focus on top-box scores rather than on top-and-middle-box scores because top-box scores drive profitability the most.

» Disregarding those benchmarks that encourage performance barely beyond mediocre and instead establishing improvement goals for engagement and retention at the organizational and leader levels.

» Conducting stay interviews as a process—on a schedule, with scripted questions, teaching leaders to listen and probe, and expecting them to develop stay plans with each employee.

» Forecasting each employee's future length of service and engagement levels to further drive leaders' commitments and accountabilities.

» Redirecting traditional exit surveys from HR to managers who consult with their supervisors on why each employee left and what could have been done to keep each of them.

Stay Out of The Moat!

Let's imagine this business-driven solution as a board game. Our board would have each of the five processes circled around the center of the board, and we would roll dice and advance from dollars to goals to stay interviews, and then to forecasting and then to accountability. Once we reached all five, we would win the game by crossing a moat into the high-spired castle of strong engagement and high retention.

But surrounding the castle is a moat. The moat contains both alligators and crocodiles along with other scary creatures. The moat represents pushback from executives and managers at all levels regarding what we are asking them to do, which is to own their talent. "Owning talent" sounds easy until we also ask them to meet on schedule in structured ways with their employees and then to be accountable for engagement, retention, and their forecasts for both.

Successfully crossing this moat is literally a life-or-death event for implementing these engagement and retention processes. Surrendering to "managers don't have time" or "it doesn't fit our culture" is waving the white flag and choosing to be gobbled up by the creatures in the moat. "HR rather than managers should conduct stay interviews" leads to the same fate.

This dilemma harkens back to Mark Jin's quote from the Introduction: "For HR executives to do this, they must have courage."

Ultimately, CEOs and their C-suite teams must be asked this question to confront the research that might run against their beliefs and even their wishes: Where do engagement and retention happen?

1. From executives on down with topside-driven programs such as CEO videos during onboarding or town hall meetings?
2. From staff divisions like HR or training with compensation, benefits, and manager skill-building?
3. From first-line leaders from the bottom up, who hire and coach their employees and their colleagues?

The correct answer, of course, is 3. And the great news is that these first-line leaders will not only fully own their talent, but they will drive change by now coming forward to say, "I must retain this high performer and to do so I need help to think outside the box, beyond our normal policies and ways we do things, to accommodate him or her to some degree."

This is the most productive, most powerful form of change because it sources directly from the most important needs of your most important employees. The speed and quality of this change flies by the typical company responses to employee surveys that assume one line of data reflects all employee opinions and that then result in months of planning and executing—if real responses occur at all.

To ensure you overcome resistance to the quiz question above, reread the section in Chapter 6 titled "Overcoming Stay Interview Objections." Stand armed and ready to present data from Chapter 1 on dollar values or from Chapter 2 on why current solutions are not really solutions.

Leader Power Examples #24 and #25

There are 25 Leader Power Examples scattered throughout this book, distributed to provide reminders of the undisputed and unwavering power immediate supervisors bring each hour to influence how hard your employees work and how long they stay. Here are two final examples for you to consider and share. The first is a personal career story, and the second in the textbox below provides straight talk on the overwhelming power leaders at all levels bring to your organization.

What has been the best day of your career? New job? Big promotion? Mine was the day my CEO told me I was accountable for turnover, that my "middle initial was now T for turnover."

I walked away frustrated because we in HR had done surveys, conducted focus groups, reevaluated compensation and benefits plans, implemented many employee programs, and had not moved the needle. We also had a hunch that leaders drove retention.

Searching for a new fix, I asked the top operations executive for help. He told me the solution was simple, that he would present turnover data to all key managers and tell them they would be held accountable for reaching a turnover goal—and that 20 percent of their bonuses would be tied to that achievement.

The outcome was that nine months later turnover was down 19 percent and the CEO thought I was a hero. My own role was limited to producing a report each month that detailed each leader's performance against his or her turnover goal. No higher pay for employees, no new training programs, no new nothing. Just goals, consequences, and an accountability report.

That day woke me up to how engagement and retention really work and to the limited role HR plays in these outcomes, and it gave me knowledge I have built on throughout my career. And I know from talking with those managers that seeing their names on reports against a goal meant far more than any bonus dollars they could win.

Our Final Leader Power Example, #25

Gallup CEO Jim Clifton has spoken out often on the roles leaders play in engaging and retaining their teams. His comments reflect his company's vast databases of research on these topics. Below is one of his overarching quotes:

> Here's something they'll probably never teach you in business school: The single biggest decision you make in your job—bigger than all the rest—is who you name manager. When you name the right people to manage your company's workplace, everything goes well. People love their jobs, your customers are engaged, and life is great. When you name the wrong person manager, nothing fixes that bad decision. Not compensation, not benefits—nothing.
>
> Of the approximately 100 million people in America who hold full-time jobs, 30 million (30 percent) are engaged and inspired at work, so we can assume they have a great boss. At the other end of the spectrum are roughly 20 million (20 percent) employees who are actively disengaged. These employees, who have bosses from hell that make them miserable, roam the halls spreading discontent. The other 50 million (50 percent) American workers are not engaged. They're just kind of present, but not inspired by their work or their managers.
>
> Gallup research also shows that these managers from hell are creating active disengagement costing the U.S. an estimated $450 billion to $550 billion annually. If your company reflects the average in the U.S., just imagine what poor management and disengagement are costing your bottom line.[1]

The Absence of Innovation

Why is it that most companies sign contracts to buy exit surveys from vendors that lead to no substantial changes? That we are pleased to barely exceed engagement and turnover benchmarks when they represent that we are just one skinny notch beyond mediocre?

Why is it that most companies hold either no one accountable or the wrong people accountable for improving engagement and retention?

How can it be that employee engagement has not substantially changed since 2000, but we continue to pour hundreds of millions of dollars into the identical solutions?

It is tempting here to describe all the ways our society has changed since 2000 while employee engagement solutions have remained both ineffective and the same. Let's identify just one. In 2000 your cellphone was just a phone, but now it is a computer. Technology companies converted our phones into computers because they saw the dollars they could make by doing so, and they established goals to get products to market to beat the competition. Consumers today so crave the next-level phone that they buy insurance to upgrade at no additional cost. Why is there not one percent of the same drive for innovation to improve engagement and retention?

Better solutions must come from vendors, academicians, or those of us who practice in the field. Vendors are thriving as they take in much of those hundreds of millions each year. Their first measure of success is growth of their own sales, so why should they change?

Academicians have produced outstanding research on topics mentioned in this book, but unfortunately few of us consult it. Their typical approach, though, is to study variations on *what has worked* rather than *what could work*, so they usually operate in the rearview mirror.

That leaves just *us* to innovate. Too many times, though, our innovation is blocked by our assumptions that our current processes result in the best we can do—like rush-hour traffic—or that the CEO will not agree to this, or that our managers would never do that. So we default to "same old."

The turnover cost calculator presented in Chapter 4 was developed by a few of us who constantly challenged each other over time, with a key ingredient contributed during a client meeting in midtown Manhattan. Retention forecasting was born in a late afternoon client session in Peoria, Illinois. The forecasting report presented here was first implemented by a technology company in a suburb of Orlando. I first heard of manager/supervisor exit interviews from a small-company CEO who lives in Portland, Oregon. All four ideas were formed because the goal was to *identify what will work* rather than to continue on the same ineffective paths or to allow ourselves to be stumped by others' potential objections.

It is clear, then, that the innovator must be *you*, whether you implement these processes just as suggested or do variations that work even better for your company.

What ... Gulp ... Do People Want the Most?

In his book *The Coming Jobs War*, Jim Clifton disclosed Gallup's highly ambitious study to learn what the 7 billion people on our planet want the most.[2] To discover the answer, Gallup has committed to its world poll by polling citizens of over 150 countries each year for a full 100 years. So far the researchers have accumulated data for six years. What would you guess is the answer to what the people want the most? Here are some possibilities:

- Good health, based on the assumption that all of our thoughts and activities are tied to our feeling and being healthy
- A good job that provides the desired amount of work
- Love and respect from others since good feelings come from

good relationships
» Money and all necessities and comforts that come with it
» Or better lives for our children since many of us devote much of our energy to those we've brought into our world

The answer so far is "a good job." Clifton went on to say that a good job "defines your relationship with your city, your country, and the whole world around you." Many of us identify strongly with our work duties, achievements, companies, and titles. And work relationships play strong roles in our social lives as many people spend more time with work colleagues than with their families.

This is big news because it represents a supportive voice from the other side, the employee side. We long for ways to better engage and retain our teams, and it now appears employees are clued into the dominant role work plays in their personal pursuits of happiness. A fair conclusion then is that all of us, or at least most of us, want the same thing.

I know with 100 percent conviction that the ideas in this book work and lead to increased productivity and happiness for all levels of managers and employees—and I look forward to hearing about your successes. In fact, feel free to e-mail me and I'll send you a PowerPoint deck of this book's highlights that you can share with your executives.

Good luck … and take care.

Dick Finnegan
DFinnegan@C-SuiteAnalytics.com

Appendix A:
The Best Engagement and Retention Job Description

Many organizations have developed one or more jobs for HR specialists to concentrate their energies on employee engagement and retention. The best of these jobs focuses on metrics and proven ways to improve them whereas other jobs take on a "kitchen sink" quality in that all employee-related activities become the responsibility of the person in this job, polluting the employee's effectiveness.

Here is an ideal job description for this position based on the contents of this book:

Title: Engagement & Retention Specialist

Reports to: Top HR Executive

Job summary: Responsible for metrics, reports, goal-setting, and survey administration; ensures stay interview completion and related forecasts are reported to management.

Specific duties:

1. Costs: Oversees development of turnover costs and engagement survey dollar values to ensure reports contain dollar data at the organizational and leader levels.

2. Goals: Ensures executives establish engagement and retention goals at least annually; engagement goals are developed for an increase in employees who score in the top box, and retention goals are established for all turnover and also for first-year turnover.

3. Turnover reports: Develops, maintains, and distributes

turnover reports at the organizational and leader levels that contain performance against annual and first-year goals and turnover costs.

4. Engagement survey administration: Ensures surveys are planned and administered according to schedule.

5. Engagement survey reports: Develops, maintains, and distributes employee engagement survey reports at the organizational and leader level and ensures reports contain the percentage of employees who score in the top box against goals as well as engagement dollar values.

6. Stay interview administration: Ensures dates are established for stay interview administration, both for continuing and newly hired employees.

7. Stay interview completion: Reviews stay interview and retention forecast completion by manager and provides exception reports to management.

8. Engagement survey correlations: Conducts or oversees the conduction of engagement survey correlation studies to determine employee engagement dollar values in relation to shareholder returns, profits, revenues, and other important metrics.

9. Engagement survey action plans: Spot-checks managers' engagement survey action plans to ensure that planned improvements are relevant to survey results and that they focus on supervisory skills more than on employee programs.

10. Action plan fulfillment: Develops process for managers to self-report their progress regarding implementing their engagement action plans.

11. New managers: Instructs new managers on their roles and reports regarding engagement and retention.

12. Counsel: Advises the top HR executive regarding issues that significantly affect engagement or retention at the organizational or leader levels.

Appendix B:
How to Solve Health Care's Unique Engagement and Retention Challenges with Doctors and Nurses

In earlier chapters I detailed the high cost of health care turnover with specific data regarding doctors and nurses. These costs are exponentially compounded by current and projected talent shortages for both jobs. To refresh, one organization found the cost of losing a physician to total $225,808, and another determined losing one nurse to be $141,000. Our experience is that this physician turnover cost is near the bottom compared to other studies, whereas the nurse amount is higher than others. You may expect, though, that each nurse who leaves your health facility costs about $50,000 or more.

The organizational structure of hospitals brings two distinct challenges for engagement and retention, so the purpose of this special section is to identify and fix them. The two issues are (a) typically no executive is accountable for doctor turnover because doctors are not treated as employees, and (b) nurse managers have far too many direct reports to build relationships with their teams.

Hospitals have a low-hanging-fruit opportunity to increase profitability by retaining the doctors who bring in most of their revenue. Because doctors are held in such esteem and have incomparable roles, their names rarely if ever appear on organization charts. Usually a chief medical officer is included, and doctors "fall under" that person, or the names of administrators who help those doctors manage their businesses are listed. But the standard methods of reporting and accountability are unclear.

Who, then, should be assigned accountability for retaining and engaging these most important employees in hospitals? The answer might be the CEO, the COO, the chief medical officer, or another top executive. Most importantly, this person must have the authority and talent to develop relationships, probe to learn real issues, and design solutions to retain doctors and motivate them to perform at their best. And the person who takes on this role must have retention goals and be held accountable.

Conduct Stay Interviews with Doctors

Many hospital executives believe taking doctors and their spouses to the country club for dinner constitutes an engagement and retention tactic when in reality the comfort-building small talk overtakes the real required conversations. The advantages to stay interviews detailed earlier apply as much to, and perhaps more to, doctors who often feel catered to in general but develop no sense of personal attachment and therefore fail to develop open relationships with hospital administrators. Asking doctors why they stay and what could help them stay longer might result in discussions regarding improved equipment, different roles, unusual benefits, or other changes we cannot anticipate. These are nuggets we would rather hear now than on their way out the door.

I have recently read articles about "what doctors want," based on surveys across the country. Isn't it easier just to ask them rather than assume they fit the mold?

Hiring and Retaining Doctors in Rural Areas

This situation is even stickier for health care organizations in rural areas, or "frontier" parts of our country as one executive recently described his location. We have worked with health care companies in Alaska and other points south that face a critical shortage of medical providers and a dearth of local talent. How, then, do they recruit and retain doctors?

Recently I participated in a roundtable discussion about ways to retain physicians in rural areas. Ideas from executives included that they hunt and fish, that they bring a spouse to avoid loneliness, and that they do not crave regular trips to shopping malls. One panelist said she set out to find her newly relocated physician a wife and succeeded, and that the wife promised to never leave the area. The discussion reminded me of *Doc Hollywood*, the clever movie in which Michael J. Fox plays a Los Angeles-bound young doctor who gets waylaid in rural South Carolina.

It is essential to require any doctor who expresses interest to make an onsite visit, and then that you tell rather than sell—and maybe even exaggerate—the disadvantages of country life by making statements like these:

» "This is our local grocery store, and you can get about anything you need here outside of a Home Depot, and we have one of those 19 miles away."

» "This lake is the area social center from June through Labor Day and especially on the Fourth of July. Our kids don't hang out in a mall here; they come to the lake."

» "Sundays are family days here. This is how we get away from work on a weekend, by having long, slow suppers together."

It is equally imperative to make these conversations 3-D. The doctor should be inside the grocery store when you tell how far away Home Depot is, at the lake when you describe a kid-filled summer day there. Or said another way, rural lifestyle must be demonstrated in ways that smack the senses.

Another important step is to advise the doctor in advance that you will schedule a meeting with a Realtor. Ask the Realtor to drive the doctor to selected properties based on the doctor's interests, and ask the Realtor to tell you later just how much the doctor seemed committed to actually moving there and perhaps buying a home.

Also during the visit, tour your health care facility and introduce the doctor to patients. Describe the common ailments and strongly emphasize the area's need for great medical care.

Then when interviewing the doctor, ask about life history and listen for hints of adaptability. Moving frequently as a child might be a sign the doctor can adjust to different environments and also make friends easily.

Be sure, also, to tell the doctor these two things:

1. The types of doctors who have enjoyed the area in the past and also the types who left early, without holding back any cause-effect reason, including lifestyle, loneliness, spouse disapproval, weather—anything

2. Tell the doctor the minimum number of years he or she should plan to stay to be fair to your community; this is not a binding commitment from either side but instead an expectation that should be clear.

The above ideas align with a hiring technique called realistic job previews. The idea is to make explicitly clear to applicants the absolute worst parts of the job before hire, so they possibly screen themselves out or send you nonverbal hints not to hire them.

One final question to ask doctors is what can be done to make their adjustment to living in your community easier. They might ask for a quarterly plane ticket to another part of the country, a club membership, or another "thing" that will be well worth your investment.

Before closing, let's look back at that "family" issue, recalling that one panel member successfully made a marriage connection for her newly recruited doctor. And—spoiler alert here—remember why Doc Hollywood ultimately left Los Angeles and returned to South Carolina. It just seems like having a partner from the start can make any lifestyle change better.

If you live in a remote area, send your doctor candidates a copy of *Doc Hollywood* before they arrive, and advise them tongue-in-cheek there will be a quiz. They will note your creativity and come with smiles on their faces.[1]

Nurse Staffing Ratios Make Engagement and Retention a Steep Uphill Climb

Managers often say they are too busy to conduct stay interviews, and nurse managers are among the loudest. The conundrum is that nurse turnover is often high and extremely expensive, and few jobs face such an extreme shortage of talent.

But nurse managers who claim busy-ness make a strong point. For whatever reason, hospital organization charts show nurse managers with way too many direct reports. One study indicated that a typical nurse manager oversees three departments and a total of 69 employees.[2] Imagine telling a manager who has 69 direct reports that he or she is accountable for engaging and retaining his or her team and must conduct at least one stay interview per year for each of the 69. Another study concluded that each nurse manager's span of control was the highest predictor of staff turnover.[3]

Hospital administrators grew up with this idea and hardly seem to question it. They believe the intervention of "charge nurses" overcomes the problem, with charge nurses being those who are designated during shifts to answer questions and maybe create the schedule. Missing in this discussion is, who is the person who will develop the nurturing relationship with each nurse to engage and retain that individual? It likely will not be the overtaxed manager, and the charge nurse is chosen for knowledge rather than for leadership skills.

Dilemmas such as this shed light on why the turnover rate for nurses fresh out of college is approximately 27 percent during their first year of employment.[4]

One solution is to revise the charge nurse job to include actual supervisory skills and therefore greatly reduce the manager/nurse ratio. Doing so might require reinterviewing incumbents to see if they fit and also raising their pay a bit. One can make a case for these costs by calculating the cost for losing a nurse and projecting lower annual turnover. Improved spans of control would likely increase patient quality and Hospital Consumer Assessment of Healthcare Providers and Systems (HCAHPS) scores too, as well as lead to fewer infections and deaths as we saw in Chapter 1.

And then these nurses can receive all the benefits provided by real supervision and stay interviews.[5]

In 30 Words or Less … The 30 Best Finnegan Quotes

1. Asking your executive team to manage engagement and retention as a top-5 metric requires courage—as does asking them to hold themselves and other leaders accountable.

2. When was the last time you heard a really good worker say, "My boss treats me like dirt, but I'm holding on for employee appreciation week"?

3. Employees stay for things they get uniquely from you. Identify this for each individual employee, leverage it, and you win.

4. Your best boss was someone you trusted, and your worst boss was someone you did not. And your best boss had shortcomings you easily accepted, whereas your worst boss had strengths you couldn't possibly see.

5. Human relationships spin on two variables, trust and self-esteem. You stick with people who are looking out for you and who make you feel good about being you.

6. By definition, 50 percent of doctors graduated in the bottom half of their classes—which means some of your managers are way better than other managers.

7. If you can think of one manager who can't build trust with his team, cancel all other efforts to improve engagement and retention until you fix this problem.

8. If you say you treat employees like customers, would you tell dissatisfied customers you have an action plan for improvement and then survey them again a full year later?

9. Retention is Goals + Tools and those tools must become Processes. And the best process is stay interviews.

10. How do you manage sales and service? Convert outcomes to dollars, establish goals, and then provide tools, solicit forecasts, and apply accountability. Manage engagement and retention just like sales and service.

11. The first step to making engagement and retention first-tier metrics is to convert survey scores and turnover percentages to the CEO language, which is dollars.

12. The best benchmarks are internal. Tell your CEO your turnover is better than your peers', and he or she will be happy. Tell your CEO how much your turnover costs, and she'll never ask about your peers' turnover rates.

13. The problem with engagement benchmarks is we aim for one step above the middle. Beating the average can make us feel very, very good about 70 percent of our employees not giving their best.

14. The #1 reason employees say they will leave is pay. The #1 reason employees say they left is pay. The #1 reason supervisors think employees leave is pay. The #1 reason why employees actually leave is their immediate supervisors.

15. Nearly all employees can look for a job with more money and find it. The question is, what did we do that made you look?

16. "Better opportunity" tells you nothing. If you permit employees to check "better opportunity" on exit surveys, stop doing the surveys and save your money.

17. Engagement surveys give data but no solutions. Managers try to solve poor communications with town hall meetings and recognition with employee-of-the-month awards. Employees just want better bosses.

18. CFOs' jobs are to find coins in the couch, and they sleep with notepads on their nightstands. If CFOs learned the real cost of turnover and disengagement, all companies would be managed better.

19. Employees work in small bubbles. They want supervisors they trust, jobs they enjoy doing, to feel challenged by their work, and have colleagues who pull their fair share. All are controlled by supervisors.

20. Studies confirm that employees stay for good bosses despite below-market pay.

21. The definition of a jerk boss is someone others do not trust. A jerk boss will overcome great pay, good benefits, or any employee program.

22. Usually pay matters most when employees feel disrespected by a jerk boss or something else unrelated to pay.

23. Workplaces are rats' nests for trust because of authority, competition, stress, and sometimes incompetence. The most important quality is also the most fragile.

24. Employee benefits have very little impact on engagement or retention.

25. In our survey, just 12 out of 6,000 HR professionals said exit surveys helped them improve their companies. What does that tell you?

26. Exit surveys are way too long. We only want to know why employees left. Who cares about their 1 to 10 score on pay, benefits, or the cafeteria?

27. Team goals mean no one is accountable. Individual goals turn diffused light into lasers.

28. Gallup is proving that the #1 key to peoples' happiness is a good job, so the good news is we all want the same thing. The responsibility is on us to provide it.

29. My favorite part in the movie *Office Space* is when Lumbergh introduces the two Bobs to his staff and then says with a flat face, "And remember, next Friday is Hawaiian shirt day."

30. My favorite movie is *Groundhog Day* because Phil Connors, Bill Murray's character, eventually makes a great situation out of a bad one—and it still makes me laugh.

Endnotes

Chapter 1

1. For example, see U.S. Bureau of Labor Statistics, "Employment Cost Index—September 2014," October 31, 2014, http://www.bls.gov/news.release/eci.nr0.htm; and Society for Human Resource Management, "SHRM Human Capital Benchmarking Study: 2007 Executive Summary," 2007, http://www.shrm.org/Research/SurveyFindings/Documents/SHRM%20Human%20Capital%20Benchmarking%20Study%202007%20Executive%20Summary.pdf.

2. Gallup, "Gallup's Employee Engagement Science," https://q12.gallup.com/Help/en-us/About.

3. Gallup, *State of the American Workplace: Employee Engagement Insights for U.S. Business Leaders*, 2013, http://www.gallup.com/file/strategicconsulting/163007/State%20of%20the%20American%20Workplace%20Report%202013.pdf.

4. Ibid, 13.

5. Ibid, 12-13.

6. Great Place to Work Institute, "Identifying Best Places to Work: U.S. and Globally," 2014, http://www.greatplacetowork.com/best-companies.

7. Great Place to Work Institute, "What Are the Benefits?" Slide: "100 Best Companies Voluntary Turnover by Industry," http://www.greatplacetowork.com/our-approach/what-are-the-benefits-great-workplaces.

8. Great Place to Work Institute, "Identifying Best Places to Work: U.S. and Globally," 2014.

9. Towers Watson, *Engagement at Risk: Driving Strong*

Performance in a Volatile Global Environment, 2012 Global Workforce Study, July 2012, http://www.towerswatson.com/ Insights/IC-Types/Survey-Research-Results/2012/07/2012-Towers-Watson-Global-Workforce-Study.

10. Rebecca R. Hastings, "Reports Link Employee Engagement and Customer Experience," Society for Human Resource Management, Oct. 29, 2012, http://www.shrm.org/ hrdisciplines/employeerelations/articles/pages/employee-engagement-customer-experience.aspx.

11. These data are taken from a report by DDI, which no longer exists. The author has a copy of the report, and it states, "Michael Treacy, author of *Double-Digit Growth-How Great Companies Achieve It No Matter What* [New York: Portfolio, 2004], worked with Hewitt Associates to demonstrate the relationship between double-digit growth and engagement." The data are reported in Chapter 1 of the book.

12. Kenexa, "Leveraging Employee Surveys to Influence Business Performance," in *Engage Ebook: Valuable Insights and Research on Employee Engagement*, 2012, 17, http://kenexa.com/ Portals/0/Downloads/Engage-e-Book.pdf.

13. Ibid.

14. Watson Wyatt, "Driving Business Results through Continuous Engagement," 2008/2009 WorkUSA Survey Report, https:// www.executestrategy.net/materials/watsonwyatt.pdf.

15. Saratoga Institute, *Driving the Bottom Line: Improving Retention*, 2006, 1, http://www.pwc.com/en_US/us/hr-saratoga/assets/saratoga-improving-retention.pdf.

16. Victor Lipman, "Study Explores Drivers of Employee Engagement," *Forbes*, December 14, 2012, http://www.forbes. com/sites/victorlipman/2012/12/14/study-explores-drivers-of-employee-engagement/.

17. Rudy Darsan, "The Real Cost of Turnover," *Kenexa Connection*, 6, no. 3.

18. Figures are based on discussions the author had with key

officials in the cited organizations.

19. U.S. Bureau of Labor Statistics, "Table A-4. Employment status of the civilian population 25 years and over by educational attainment," October 2014, http://www.bls.gov/news.release/empsit.t04.htm.

20. Allen Smith, "Microsoft General Counsel: Talent Shortage is Getting Worse," Society for Human Resource Management, Sept. 28, 2012, http://www.shrm.org/legalissues/federalresources/pages/stem-talent-shortage.aspx.

21. Elizabeth Craig et al, *Where Will All the STEM Talent Come From?*, May 2012, 3, http://www.accenture.com/SiteCollectionDocuments/PDF/Accenture-Where-Will-All-the-STEM-Talent-Come-From-FINAL.pdf.

22. Ibid, 5.

23. "Salary Survey: Top-Paid Majors for the Class of 2014," National Association of Colleges and Employers, April 16, 2014, https://www.naceweb.org/s04162014/top-paid-majors-class-of-2014.aspx.

24. Kurt Mosley, "New Survey Reveals the Revenue Physicians and Recruiters Generate for Their Hospitals," *Recruiting Trends*, http://www.recruitingtrends.com/thought-leadership/77-new-survey-reveals-the-revenue-physicians-and-recruiters-generate-for-their-hospitals. Note that the figures are rounded up.

25. Sally Pipes, "Thanks to Obamacare, A 20,000 Doctor Shortage is Set to Quintuple," *Forbes*, June 10, 2013, http://www.forbes.com/sites/sallypipes/2013/06/10/thanks-to-obamacare-a-20000-doctor-shortage-is-set-to-quintuple.

26. U.S. Bureau of Labor Statistics, "Table 6. Employment by major occupational group, 2012 and Projected 2022," http://www.bls.gov/news.release/ecopro.t06.htm.

27. "New AACN Data Show an Enrollment Surge in Baccalaureate and Graduate Programs Amid Calls for More Highly Educated Nurses," American Association of Colleges of Nursing, Mar. 22, 2012, http://www.aacn.nche.edu/news/articles/2012/

enrollment-data.

28. Ibid.

29. "Nurses and Hospital Employees' Top Concerns: Communication, Staffing and Compensation," PR Newswire, Oct. 24, 2007, http://www.prnewswire.com/news-releases/ nurses-and-hospital-employees-top-concerns-communication-staffing-and-compensation-58880642.html.

30. "Nursing Shortage Fact Sheet," American Association of Colleges of Nursing, Apr. 24, 2014, http://www.aacn.nche. edu/media-relations/NrsgShortageFS.pdf.

31. Dale Buss, "A Renaissance for American Manufacturing?" *Chief Executive*, Sept. 14, 2012, http://chiefexecutive.net/a-renaissance-for-american-manufacturing2.

32. Ibid.

33. Ed Frauenheim, "Bringing the Jobs Back Home: How 'Re-shoring' Is Coming to America," Feb. 7, 2013, http://www. workforce.com/articles/bringing-the-jobs-back-home-how-re-shoring-is-coming-to-america.

34. Rick Jervis and Jon Swartz, "Google, at 15, Perfects Search for the Next Big Thing," *USA Today*, September 26, 2013, http:// usat.ly/1apwUxY.

35. Deloitte, *Boiling Point?: The Skills Gap in U.S. Manufacturing*, 2011, http://www.themanufacturinginstitute.org/~/media/A0 7730B2A798437D98501E798C2E13AA.ashx.

36. "Current Issues in HR: Closing the Manufacturing Skills Gap," SHRM Foundation Executive Briefing, 2013, 1, https://www. shrm.org/about/foundation/products/Documents/4-13%20 Skills%20Gap%20Briefing.pdf.

37. Ibid, 1-2.

38. Ibid, 1.

39. Ibid, 2.

40. Mark Puente, "A Shortage of Drivers has Trucking Companies Offering to Pay Recruits while They're Training," *Tampa Bay Times*, Aug. 12, 2011, http://www.tampabay.com/news/

business/workinglife/a-shortage-of-drivers-has-trucking-companies-offering-to-pay-recruits/1185804.

41. "Now Hiring Bus Drivers," *Orlando Sentinel*, Nov. 25, 2012.

42. Nick Leiber, "China Makes America's Fireworks by Hand. This Inventor Has a Faster Way," *Bloomberg BusinessWeek*, July 1, 2013, http://www.businessweek.com/articles/2013-07-01/china-makes-america-s-fireworks-by-hand-dot-this-inventor-has-a-faster-way.

43. Prashant Gopal, "Arizona's New Housing Crisis: No Workers," *Bloomberg BusinessWeek*, June 28, 2012, http://www.businessweek.com/articles/2012-06-28/arizonas-new-housing-crisis-no-workers.

44. OECD, "OECD Skills Outlook 2013: First Results from the Survey of Adult Skills," November 2013, http://skills.oecd.org/documents/OECD_Skills_Outlook_2013.pdf.

45. George Anders, "How LinkedIn Has Turned Your Resume into a Cash Machine," *Forbes*, June 27, 2012, http://www.forbes.com/forbes/2012/0716/feature-linkedin-jeff-weiner-resume-other-social-network.html.

46. Ibid.

47. Ibid.

48. Fred Coon, *Leveraging LinkedIn: For Job Search Success 2014* (Self-published. Printed by CreateSpace, 2014).

49. Anders, "How LinkedIn Has Turned Your Resume into a Cash Machine."

50. George Anders, "The Other Social Network," *Forbes*, July 16, 2012.

51. Ibid.

52. Ibid.

Chapter 2

1. Gallup, *State of the American Workplace: Employee Engagement Insights for U.S. Business Leaders*, 2013, http://www.gallup.com/services/178514/state-american-workplace.aspx.

2. Ibid.

3. Ibid, 8.

4. Richard S. Wellins, Paul Bernthal, and Mark Phelps, "Employee Engagement: The Key To Realizing Competitive Advantage," Development Dimensions International, 2005, 1, https://www.ddiworld.com/DDIWorld/media/monographs/employeeengagement_mg_ddi.pdf?ext=.pdf.

5. Brenda Kowske, *Employee Engagement: Market Review, Buyer's Guide and Provider Profiles* (Oakland, CA: Bersin by Deloitte, 2012).

6. Bersin by Deloitte, "Bersin & Associates First-Ever Employee Engagement Solution Provider Buyer's Guide Identifies Latest Trends in a Fast-Growing $1.53 Billion Market," news release, August 14, 2012, https://www.bersin.com/News/Content.aspx?id=15735.

7. Jack W. Wiley, *Strategic Employee Surveys: Evidence-Based Guidelines for Driving Organizational Success* (San Francisco: Jossey-Bass, 2010), p. 5.

8. PricewaterhouseCoopers, *Engaging Your Pivotal Talent*, 2011, 6, http://www.pwc.com/gx/en/hr-management-services/assets/engaging-pivotal-talent.pdf.

9. Carol Kinsey Goman, *The Truth about Lies in the Workplace: How to Spot Liars and What to Do About Them* (San Francisco: Berrett-Koehler, 2013).

10. Personal conversation with the author, Nov. 14, 2013.

11. Confidential e-mail communication with the author on Aug. 12, 2014.

12. Finnegan/Mackenzie and ExecuNet, Inc., *2010 Executive Retention Report: Executives Discreetly Exploring Career Options: And Why the Boss Doesn't Know*, 2010, http://www.execunet.com/promo/pdf/ExecuNet_R_Executive_Retention_Report_Finnegan_2010.pdf.

Chapter 3

1. See U.S. Bureau of Labor Statistics, "Employment Cost Index—September 2014," October 31, 2014, http://www.bls.gov/news.release/eci.nr0.htm; and Society for Human Resource Management, "SHRM Human Capital Benchmarking Study: 2007 Executive Summary," 2007, http://www.shrm.org/Research/SurveyFindings/Documents/SHRM%20Human%20Capital%20Benchmarking%20Study%202007%20Executive%20Summary.pdf.

2. The Economist Intelligence Unit, *CFO Perspectives: How HR Can Take on a Bigger Role in Driving Growth*, 2012, http://www.oracle.com/us/c-central/cfo-solutions/eiu-ibm-oracle-cfo-report-1877303.pdf.

3. Jeffrey S. Sanders, "The Path to Becoming a Fortune 500 CEO," *Forbes*, Dec. 5, 2011, http://www.forbes.com/sites/ciocentral/2011/12/05/the-path-to-becoming-a-fortune-500-ceo/.

4. Temkin Group, "CX Needs More HR Focus on Employee Engagement," Sept. 2012, http://www.temkingroup.com/research-reports/cx-needs-more-hr-focus-on-employee-engagement/; and Rebecca R. Hastings, "Reports Link Employee Engagement and Customer Experience," Society for Human Resource Management, Oct. 29, 2012, http://www.shrm.org/hrdisciplines/employeerelations/articles/pages/employee-engagement-customer-experience.aspx.

5. Bersin by Deloitte, "Bersin & Associates First-Ever Employee Engagement Solution Provider Buyer's Guide."

6. Employee Turnover Trends Report by TalentKeepers, 2007.

7. The Economist Intelligence Unit, *CFO Perspectives*.

8. "100 Best Companies to Work For: 2012," *Fortune*, http://archive.fortune.com/magazines/fortune/best-companies/2012/snapshots/1.html.

9. "100 Best Companies to Work For: 2013," *Fortune*, http://archive.fortune.com/magazines/fortune/best-

companies/2013/snapshots/1.html.

10. "100 Best Companies to Work For: 2014: Google," http://fortune.com/best-companies/2014/.

11. "100 Best Companies to Work For: 2015: Google," http://fortune.com/best-companies/google-1/.

12. "100 Best Companies to Work For: How We Pick the 100 Best Companies," *Fortune*, http://archive.fortune.com/magazines/fortune/best-companies/2014/methodology/.

13. Great Place to Work Institute, "Trust Index(c) Employee Survey," 2014, http://www.greatplacetowork.com/our-services/assess-your-organization.

14. Ibid.

15. Great Place to Work Institute, "Identifying Best Places to Work: U.S. and Globally," 2014, http://www.greatplacetowork.com/best-companies.

Chapter 4

1. Gallup, *State of the American Workplace: Employee Engagement Insights for U.S. Business Leaders*, 2013, downloadable at http://www.gallup.com/file/strategicconsulting/163007/State%20of%20the%20American%20Workplace%20Report%202013.pdf. See also Figure 2.1.

2. Bill Chafetz, Robin Adair Erickson, and Josh Ensell, "Where Did Our Employees Go? Examining the Rise in Voluntary Turn Over during Economic Recoveries," *Deloitte Review*, January 20, 2011, http://www.deloitte.com/view/en_US/us/Insights/Browse-by-Content-Type/deloitte-review/f506d5ce78ea2210VgnVCM200000bb42f00aRCRD.htm citing Corporate Leadership Council, *Driving Employee Performance and Retention through Engagement: A Quantitative Analysis of the Effectiveness of Employee Engagement Strategies*, 2004, Washington DC: Corporate Executive Board.

3. Salary.com, *Employee Job Satisfaction & Retention Survey, 2007/2008: An Employer versus Employee Overview*, http://

www.salary.com/docs/resources/JobSatSurvey_08.pdf.

4. "Study: School Systems Testing New Teacher Retention Strategies," *SHRM Staffing Management News*, August 2007.

5. Craig R. Taylor, "The Tides of Talent," T+D, 57, no. 4 (April 2003).

6. Richard P. Finnegan, "Retention Corner," *Recruiting Trends*, May 22, 2007.

7. The initials PRN stand for the Latin phrase *pro re nata*, which means "as the situation demands."

8. Ernest O'Boyle Jr. and Herman Aguinis, "The Best and the Rest: Revisiting the Norm of Normality of Individual Performance," *Personnel Psychology*, Spring 2012, 65:1, 79-119; and John Sullivan, "Top Performers Produce 4X More Output and Higher Quality Referrals," ere.net, May 6, 2013, http://www.ere.net/2013/05/06/top-performers-produce-4x-more-output-and-higher-quality-referrals/.

9. Frederick F. Reichheld, *The Loyalty Effect: The Hidden Force Behind Growth, Profits, and Lasting Value* (Boston: Harvard Business School Press, 1996), 98.

10. "Putting the Service-Profit Chain to Work," Money Watch, July 18, 2008, www.cbsnews.com/news/putting-the-service-profit-chain-to-work.

11. Clifton Gott, Debra Schmitt, and Gerald E. Ledford Jr., "Manage Turnover to Boost Retention," Contact Professional, Jan. 1, 2003, http://www.contactprofessional.com/topics/managing-motivating/manage-turnover-and-boost-retention-529.

12. Watson Wyatt, "Debunking the Myths of Employee Engagement," WorkUSA Survey Report, 2007.

13. Ibid.

14. The employee turnover calculator and employee engagement calculators referenced here are available for use at www.C-SuiteAnalytics.com. By inserting data the calculators provide all dollar outcomes that you can then include in turnover and engagement survey reports. To inquire about using them, please

contact us via this site.

15. Delivered via e-mail from Dr. Gary Borich to the author.

16. PricewaterhouseCoopers, "Delivering Results: Growth and Value in a Volatile World," 15th Annual Global CEO Survey, 2012, http://www.pwc.com/gx/en/ceo-survey/pdf/15th-global-pwc-ceo-survey.pdf.

17. The Economist Intelligence Unit, *CFO Perspectives: How HR Can Take on a Bigger Role in Driving Growth*, 2012, http://www.oracle.com/us/c-central/cfo-solutions/eiu-ibm-oracle-cfo-report-1877303.pdf.

Chapter 5

1. Advisory Board Company, *Hardwiring Right Retention: Best Practices for Retaining a High Performance Workforce* (Washington, DC: Advisory Board Company, 2001).

2. "Retention Strategies for 2006 and Beyond," Monster Intelligence, Winter 2006. Available at https://www.shrm.org/Publications/hrmagazine/EditorialContent/Documents/Monster_Research_Retention_Strategies_for_2006.pdf.

3. National Commission on Teaching and America's Future, *The Cost of Teacher Turnover in Five School Districts: A Pilot Study*, 2007, http://files.eric.ed.gov/fulltext/ED497176.pdf.

4. Kenexa Research Institute, *Should I Stay or Should I Go?* (Armonk, NY: Kenexa Research Institute, 2007).

5. Ann Howard et al, *Employee Retention in China 2006/2007: The Flight of Human Talent*, Development Dimensions International and the Society for Human Resource Management, http://www.shrm.org/research/surveyfindings/documents/2006-2007%20employee%20retention%20in%20china.pdf.

6. Richard P. Finnegan, *Rethinking Retention in Good Times and Bad: Breakthrough Ideas for Keeping Your Best Workers* (Mountain View, CA: Davies-Black Publishers and Alexandria, VA: Society for Human Resource Management, 2009).

Chapter 6

1. Richard P. Finnegan, *Rethinking Retention in Good Times and Bad: Breakthrough Ideas for Keeping Your Best Workers* (Mountain View, CA: Davies-Black Publishers and Alexandria, VA: Society for Human Resource Management, 2009).

2. Richard P. Finnegan, *The Power of Stay Interviews for Engagement and Retention* (Alexandria, VA: Society for Human Resource Management, 2012).

3. Kathy Gurchiek, "Research Shows Five Ways to Gain Workers' Trust," SHRM Online News, April 11, 2007.

4. Walker Information, *The Walker Loyalty Report for Loyalty in the Workplace*, September 2007, http://www.walkerinfo.com/employeeloyalty.

5. Wallace Immen, "Boomers, Gen-Yers Agree: It's All About Respect," *Globe and Mail*, Jan. 24, 2007, http://www.theglobeandmail.com/report-on-business/boomers-gen-yers-agree-its-all-about-respect/article960535.

6. Adam Bryant, "Google's Quest to Build a Better Boss," *New York Times*, Mar. 12, 2011, http://www.nytimes.com/2011/03/13/business/13hire.html?pagewanted=all&_r=0.

7. Ibid.

8. Richard P. Finnegan, "Retention Corner," *Recruiting Trends*, May 22, 2007.

9. Mary Murcott's address to her managers, August 19, 2010.

Chapter 7

1. Carey K. Morewedge and Eva C. Buechel, "Motivated Underpinnings of the Impact Bias in Affective Forecasting," *Emotion*, Dec. 2013, 13(6):1023-29.

2. "Predicting Employee Engagement," Development Dimensions International, Inc., 2005, http://66.179.232.89/pdf/ddi_selectionengagement_rr.pdf.

3. U.S. Merit Systems Protection Board, *The Power of Federal*

Employee Engagement, September 2008, www.mspb.gov/netsearch/viewdocs.aspx?docnumber=379024&version=379721&application=ACROBAT.

4. ASTD Research, *Learning's Role in Employee Engagement* (Alexandria, VA: American Society for Training and Development, 2008).

5. See Jim Jenkins, "Hint: If You're a New Manager, It's Not All About You," Society for Human Resource Management, 2006.

Chapter 8

1. Tiffany M. Greene-Shortridge and Lisa Wager, *The Role of a Person-Supervisor Fit on Employee Attitudes and Retention: Analyzing the Relationship between Employees and Their Work Environment*, IBM Software Thought Leadership Whitepaper, February 2014, http://public.dhe.ibm.com/common/ssi/ecm/en/low14191usen/LOW14191USEN.PDF.

2. "What Managers Want for 2008: A New Boss!" Yahoo! Hotjobs, Accessed August 25, 2008.

3. Ty Kiisel, "65% Of Americans Choose a Better Boss Over a Raise—Here's Why," *Forbes*, October 18, 2012, http://www.forbes.com/sites/tykiisel/2012/10/16/65-of-americans-choose-a-better-boss-over-a-raise-heres-why.

4. Marcus Buckingham and Curt Coffman, *First, Break All the Rules: What the World's Greatest Managers Do Differently* (New York: Simon & Schuster, 1999), 32.

5. Many hiring tactics to improve retention are included in my previous book, *Rethinking Retention in Good Times and Bad: Breakthrough Ideas for Keeping Your Best Workers* (Mountain View, CA: Davies-Black Publishers and Alexandria, VA: Society for Human Resource Management, 2009).

Chapter 9

1. Gallup, *State of the American Workplace: Employee Engagement Insights for U.S. Business Leaders*, 2013, http://www.gallup.

com/file/strategicconsulting/163007/State%20of%20the%20
American%20Workplace%20Report%202013.pdf.

2. Jim Clifton, *The Coming Jobs War* (Princeton, NJ: Gallup Press, 2011), 11-12.

Appendix B

1. Richard P. Finnegan, "The Secret to Recruiting and Retaining Doctors in Rural Areas is 'Watch This Movie!'," Health Callings, 2012, http://marketing.dice.com/hc_rc/whitepapers/rural_doctors/rural_doctors.html.

2. ChrysMarie Suby, "How Many Employees Can Nurse Managers Manage—While Maintaining Quality Care?" Healthcare Financial Management Association, February 1, 2010, http://www.hfma.org/Content.aspx?id=3803.

3. Amy McCutcheon and Ruth Anne Campbell, "Leadership, Span of Control, Turnover, Staff & Patient Satisfaction," paper presented to the Sigma Theta Tau International Honor Society of Nursing conference, July 16, 2005, Overview at https://stti.confex.com/stti/inrc16/techprogram/paper_23430.htm.

4. Ibid.

5. Richard P. Finnegan, "How Much Staff Turnover is OK Because of Extreme Manager/Nurse Staff Ratios?" Health Callings, http://marketing.dice.com/hc_rc/staffing_ratios.html.

Index

About the Author

Dick Finnegan has been cited by *BusinessWeek*, *Chief Executive* magazine, and *Consulting* magazine as a leading thinker on employee retention.

Dick is the CEO of C-Suite Analytics (www.C-SuiteAnalytics.com), which helps organizations engage and retain their employees. He is also the author of the bestselling *The Power of Stay Interviews for Engagement and Retention* (SHRM, 2012) and *Rethinking Retention in Good Times and Bad* (Davies-Black/SHRM, 2010). Additionally, AMACOM recently published his stay interview handbook for managers titled *The Stay Interview, A Manager's Guide for Keeping the Best and Brightest.*

His U.S. clients have included Sprint, Hilton, The Hartford, GE, and Johnson & Johnson, as well as the CIA. His international work has spanned six continents and includes working with Siberian banks as well as with African gold mines where he traveled three kilometers deep to learn why employees stay and leave. He also partners with the Chinese HR Excellence Center to conduct employee retention programs across China.

Dick is a humorous, in-demand keynote speaker for conferences and organizations. He holds undergraduate and graduate degrees from The Pennsylvania State University and lives in Orlando, Florida, where the *Orlando Sentinel* newspaper published an editorial recognizing him for his extensive donations of professional services to nonprofit organizations.

More information regarding Dick and his company is available at www.C-SuiteAnalytics.com

Additional SHRM-Published Books

The ACE Advantage: How Smart Companies Unleash Talent for Optimal Performance,
William A. Schiemann

Business-Focused HR: 11 Processes to Drive Results
Scott P. Mondore, Shane S. Douthitt, and Marisa A. Carson

The Chief HR Officer: Defining the New Role of Human Resource Leaders
Edited by Patrick M. Wright, John W. Boudreau, David A. Pace, Elizabeth "Libby" Sartain, Paul McKinnon, and Richard L. Antoine

Defining HR Success: 9 Critical Competencies for HR Professionals
Kari R. Strobel, James N. Kurtessis, Deb Cohen, and Alexander Alonso

Destination Innovation: HR's Role in Charting the Course
Patricia M. Buhler

Employee Surveys That Work: Improving Design, Use, and Organizational Impact
Alec Levenson

Got A Solution? HR Approaches to 5 Common and Persistent Business Problems
Dale J. Dwyer and Sheri A. Caldwell

Hidden Drivers of Success: Leveraging Employee Insights for Strategic Advantage
William A. Schiemann, Jerry H. Seibert, and Brian S. Morgan

HR at Your Service: Lessons from Benchmark Service Organizations
Gary P. Latham and Robert C. Ford

Human Capital Benchmarking
Society for Human Resource Management

Proving the Value of HR: How and Why to Measure ROI
Jack J. Phillips and Patricia Pulliam Phillips

Transformational Diversity: Why and How Intercultural Competencies Can Help Organizations to Survive and Thrive
Fiona Citkin and Lynda Spielman

All of SHRM's books and e-books can be found at www.shrm.org/publications/books/pages/shrm-publishedbooks(alphalist).aspx.